A Light in My Heart

YOUNG WOO KANG

John Knox Press
ATLANTA

Library of Congress Cataloging in-Publication Data

Kang, Young Woo, 1944-
  A light in my heart.

  1. Kang, Young Woo, 1944-   . 2. Presbyterians—
Biography. 3. Blind—Biography. I. Title.
BX9225.K36A3   1987   285'.13 [B]   87-2694
ISBN 0-8042-0921-9

© copyright John Knox Press 1987
10 9 8 7 6 5 4 3 2 1
Printed in the United States of America
John Knox Press
Atlanta, Georgia 30365

Preface

DR. YOUNG WOO KANG presents an example of a great victory over suffering in a single life in Korea. Born in 1944, Dr. Kang later became blind and lived in severe poverty. Yet by age 40, he had achieved brilliant victories over unimaginable trials and adversities.

Dr. Kang, speaking as a Christian, says, "God has a definite plan for my life. Even in the painful loss of my eyesight and the unhappy days of my childhood, God's divine purpose was clear. By using me as an example of tenacity, God has been glorified." Expressing his attitude toward the future, he has said, "My blindness will not remain a simple sign of darkness. Instead, it will serve as a symbol of light as I grow to full maturity in the life God has given me. Thus, my blindness performs the role of light in my life."

Dr. Kang has shown outstanding ability as a scholar of special education. He has conducted research, has taught in the United States and Korea, and has been declared one of the leading administrative consultants on practical problems in the field.

That he is also an emerging social leader I witnessed last year, when I took Dr. Kang to the Chongsong Penitentiary in Korea where he spoke with hundreds of prisoners. I saw a miracle taking place in stubborn hearts as many, strongly impressed by Dr. Kang's story of success in spite of travail and adversity, made up their minds to rehabilitate themselves.

His story, like those of Helen Keller, Gandhi, and Kagawa, gives encouragement to those who hope the twenty-first century will be a beautiful, peaceful, and discrimination-free era. Greatly appreciating the honor of writing this preface, I feel sure that in this book is living material for a brighter future.

Tae Young Rhee
President, Taegu University

Acknowledgments

THE AUTHOR expresses his sincere thanks to God for having answered his prayers by revealing the purpose of his suffering and pain.

He wishes to extend his deep appreciation to his benefactors, to those referred to as "God's people" and "human angels" in this book. He would like to name each and every one of them, but there are too many. He was reborn through their special gifts, which were as important as blood transfusions to a dying person. Their love and help have been the endless source of his energy and hope. It is by their love, commitment, and compassion toward human life that he has been able to master the darkness.

A special word of gratitude goes to his wife Kyoung. He is very proud that she is his life partner and the mother of his children. Her dedication, friendship, and commitment to family have brought a special quality to his life.

He especially acknowledges the time and talent donated to this book by Mr. William Chapman, executive editor of the *Times* of Hammond, Indiana, and editorial director of Howard Publications, Oceanside, California, who spent endless hours editing and retyping this manuscript, making many revisions and improvements; and by Mrs. Elsie McNeill, Mr. William Powell, and Mrs. Catharine Craig who provided valuable information which became an integral part of this book.

Contents

*To all my benefactors
and special friends who
made my dream come true.*

Introduction
by Elsie Griffith McNeill

TWENTY-FOUR YEARS ago Sun Hee Lee, a social worker from Korea, spent two months in training at Goodwill Industries in Los Angeles. Remembering how much we enjoyed visiting a home in a foreign country, we invited her to spend a weekend with us.

She watched closely as I prepared dinner, saying she needed to learn to cook American foods. Support for starting a Goodwill Industries in her country would have to come from housewives, and she knew women would attend any meeting that promised a demonstration of American cooking. "Then," I said, "you need something quickly prepared that is attractive and tasty." She agreed, and I added to our menu fried apples and onions, a family favorite handed down from my Pennsylvania Dutch great-great-grandmother. The red skins and tart flavor of Rome Beauty apples with a bit of sugar made it an ideal dish.

I asked Sun Hee about the children our military men had fathered in Korea. She said they were fairly well cared for because of the generosity of Americans. However, full-blooded Korean orphans were suffering because their government had no money with which to help them.

Every magazine I read at that time had pleas for adoptive parents for foreign children, and Frazier and I had agreed we could and should adopt such a child, but neither had made a move to take on this added financial responsibility. I asked Sun Hee if she knew of a particular child in need and she replied, "Yes, I do. Oh, I do! He's on my mind all the time."

She had met Young Woo Kang when he was brought to the hospital where she worked; he had attempted suicide after losing his eyesight. It was her first day on a new job, and he resolutely refused to talk. She sat beside him thinking of her desk piled with a backlog of work and finally, completely frustrated, returned to her office, telling him to call when he was ready to talk. When he left the hospital, he sought faith healing.

Almost two years later he returned to Sun Hee Lee's office, and she enrolled him in the National School for the Blind. Here for the first time he began to find a reason for living. The building was old with narrow halls and stairways bordered by rough walls. Since he still had a little sight, he was able to lead completely sightless classmates until they learned to find their way. The lad had no money and no place to go during vacations. Before leaving, she gave us the name and address of Young Woo Kang.

That conversation occurred in May 1963. During the next three months I tried many times to write letters to Young Woo but always tossed them in the wastebasket, feeling guilty as I thought of this helpless lad. Letter writing had always been one of my best talents, but now the words would not come, and I was puzzled. Finally, one day in September I wrote a letter and put it in the mail.

Two years later Soon Kwi Kwon, one of Young Woo's friends and supporters, spent a week with us on her way to New York. One day she said, "It was strange. After the funds raised by my Girl Scout troop ran out, I helped Young Woo. Then my brother was unemployed, and I had to keep his two boys in school. The hardest thing I ever had to do was tell Young Woo that I could no longer help him. In less than a month he came to tell me not to worry about him—he had parents in the United States."

A teacher read our letters to him. He took them down in Braille, then dictated a letter which the teacher wrote in longhand.

We wondered how much was lost in the dictation, and we soon had an idea. About a year later Young Woo visited a friend at the Red Cross and used her typewriter to type us a letter in much better English than his teachers had used. For Christmas 1965, we sent money for his own English typewriter, and from then on our communication was direct.

In the tenth grade his report card grades soared above ninety, and we knew we had adopted a brain. He wrote, "I am surprised that I have become a serious student." Soon he was asking if he should go to college—his teachers were encouraging him to do so. He began to attend "the Institute" during vacation periods, restricting himself to two meals a day to save money. Our Korean friends assured us this was most necessary for anyone trying to pass college entrance exams, especially to the best colleges. They said, "It puts on the polish." Every vacation until he took the exams found him studying at the Institute, a college preparatory school that prepared students for college entrance exams, and we gladly picked up the tab.

We had gone into this project thinking of $10, $15, or even $25 a month through high school with perhaps some trade training. However, we learned of the plight of the handicapped, especially the unsighted in Korea, through friends from Korea and an engineer friend who, while in Korea on business, visited Young Woo. To meet a blind person is to have bad luck the rest of the day. Blind people were occasionally pushed out of the bus, for there surely would be an accident were they allowed to ride. The engineer made enemies in Korea by asking, "Where are your handicapped? You have had a war and I know you have handicapped people. Where are you hiding them?" Sometimes the answer was that transportation was inadequate or that family concern kept the handicapped at home, but other times the individual became very emotional and could not answer.

By this time we knew Young Woo had an iron will, an excellent speaking voice, and a brilliant mind—the only combination that could possibly penetrate the massive walls of prejudice. Many times during the next six years when another barrier or insult dampened his spirit, I reminded him he was knocking down walls not just for himself but for all handicapped in Korea.

As he neared the end of the eleventh grade, he wrote asking for $400 with which to rent a room for his senior year. The school gradually weaned students from total care to independence by taking away dormitory privileges the first semester and lunchroom privileges the rest of the year. He said he would get the $400 back when he gave up the room.

"Now that boy really is pulling our leg," I exploded to Frazier, but we called the Choys who were always there to explain and who kept us from making too many blunders. "Yes," said Mr. Choy, "that is the way it is done. When you rent an apartment you may pay $1,000 down and when you move out a few years later it is returned to you. The interest rate there is 2.5 to 5 percent per month, so the landlord makes more from the interest than he can charge in rent." We sent the $400.

In 1966 Young Woo had a visit from his younger sister, Won Sook, who was in a Buddhist orphanage a few miles from Seoul. Because of her high grades she was allowed to ride a bus to Seoul to attend middle school; this was unusual since orphans rarely went beyond the elementary grades. Soon the head of the orphanage became ill, the orphanage was closed, and the orphans were moved to an orphanage far away. Won Sook moved in with friends who were willing to have her live with them but who could not afford to feed and clothe her. About that time the student government of the junior high school where I was financial manager asked me to find a child, preferably a baby, whom they could support. I told them I would find a baby if that was their wish, but I already knew a needy child in Korea who was about their age and grade. Someone with whom they might correspond appealed to them, and they supported Won Sook for the next four years. Frazier and I supported her through her senior year and two years in junior college.

Young Woo was interested only in the two top universities and preferred Yonsei. Yonsei was tougher on entrance exams, but Young Woo was determined. Transportation, however, was a problem. Buses were overcrowded, and certainly no one would help a blind person on and off. He had to live within walking distance.

When the Communists invaded Korea from the north, Young Woo's parents hid ministers and church officials, helping them escape certain death. It was to one of those ministers Young Woo turned with his problem. The Reverend Kim wrote us that he had spent his entire vacation searching the Yonsei area for a room someone would rent to a blind student. He suggested that buying a house would be the best solution. Young Woo had written about a two-year-old house which was for sale for $1,500 and was a ten-minute walk from the university. We sent a second $400 to cover increased rent in that area, giving him a total of $800, but in order to close the deal he needed $750 more.

Frazier was a staff member of the Los Angeles Goodwill Industries and had been building a scale model of a building project planned by the company. He worked on it evenings, weekends, and part of his vacation, and Goodwill paid him $500 for his time. We added the $250 still needed, and Young Woo bought the house, which turned out to be a top-notch investment. Almost immediately, inflation in Korea took an unbelievable spurt. Two months later the investment was worth $2,000. Without that home there was no way to keep Young Woo in college and have a home for all three children as circumstances changed for each. They rented out one room and with the money hired a maid—at that time a house left unattended was a house robbed. It would have been impossible for Won Sook to keep house and maintain the necessary grades to stay in school.

Entrance exams for Yonsei University were given on two consecutive days in January 1968. Applicants were tested for ninety minutes on each subject, but Young Woo was given an additional thirty minutes on each part of the test. On the second day, however, this time was rescinded with no reason given. He was expecting the additional thirty minutes on each of the remaining examinations, and the lack of it prevented him from completing the math text. He did finish the history examination, even without the additional time. Since he did not complete all the tests, he thought he had failed.

During the next two weeks I kept the letters going daily, suggesting alternatives which he promptly rejected. I always assured him that when God closes one door, God opens a better one. I was afraid that a suicide attempt now would likely succeed. I called Mrs. Choy almost daily for suggestions. One day she told me, "That boy is so lucky to have you for parents. No Korean parent could give him such support at a time like this. In Korea education is the most important aspect of a child's life, and when anything goes wrong in a child's progress, the whole family is crushed." She said suicides were not uncommon at examination time, and she confessed that she herself had always felt ill and could not eat during examination time.

Our apprehension disappeared when we received this letter: "Dear Mom and Dad: With your love and prayers I have scored tenth place. Now I have to go for the oral. Please send $260 for tuition."

Young Woo had earlier written that more than three hundred students were taking the entrance exams, but only the top thirty would be admitted. When he had applied for admission, newspapers had had a ball. Huge headlines read: GUESS WHAT! A BLIND BOY WANTS TO ENTER YONSEI! Two weeks later our friends reported even larger headlines, which read: HE PASSED! THE BLIND BOY GOT 10TH PLACE! They were loud in praise of his courage and ability.

Those four years were not easy ones. Every new class brought the same professorial response, "I don't know how to teach you. I don't want you in my class." To their credit, however, professors offered to help in any way after the first exam. Physical education teachers once refused to grade him because he could not participate in sports. That cost him first place at graduation, but he had a firm hold on second.

My greatest help to Young Woo was in English vocabulary. As soon as he began talking about college and, in the next breath, about coming to the United States, I began feeding him new words in every letter. I began expressing a thought in two or three ways, and I was rewarded when he and his bride arrived here in 1972. Knowing they had been on a plane for about thirteen hours, I asked if he had slept, and he replied, "No, I was too apprehensive." Many foreign students we had known had been here two years or more and could not express themselves nearly as well. During the week with us he made three speeches: at our church, at an interdenominational meeting where he spoke extemporaneously, and at Frazier's Rotary Club. On each occasion he tailored his speech to the particular group, and he paced the third speech to the last second of the time allowed.

Of the Girl Scouts in Miss Kwon's troop, one had continued her interest in Young Woo after the troop disbanded. They called each other brother and sister, and when the orphanage closed it was Kyoung Sook and her mother who took Won Sook into their home. Kyoung Sook then left for the United States to spend a year in training at various schools and institutions for the blind in the East and Midwest. In his senior year at Yonsei, Young Woo wrote that he and Kyoung Sook wanted to be married. We feared they might be confusing compassion and gratitude for love, but they felt they truly loved each other. We finally concluded that they were not making a rash decision and gave them our blessings.

When they arrived in the fall of 1972, I marveled that Kyoung Sook "clung" to Young Woo's arm as if he were leading her, when in reality she was guiding him. They had ridden buses all over Seoul by this clever stratagem, never once being caught. She now teaches mobility training to unsighted students and has completed her masters degree in elementary education. They are a busy family. We in our seventies are exhausted just thinking of the boys' school, sports, music, and church activities—and overtime assignments for both parents.

Young Woo's trips to Korea every summer enable us to see him almost every year and the rest of the family every two or three years. It always amazes us that he can walk into the airport terminal upon his return from Korea and dial one phone number after another, calling his friends. Physical eyes he does not have, but a photographic memory stores an unbelievable amount of knowledge, which he seems to retrieve without effort.

Sightseeing with Young Woo and his family is fun. He never seems bored when he does not know what is happening. Kyoung Sook and sons Paul and Chris cue him in, and we try to help now and then. He seems to absorb joy from the reactions of those about him. His sense of humor, especially where he himself is concerned, is refreshing. Many times he had written us of misconceptions or misunderstandings that placed him in embarrassing situations at school or out with friends, always rejoicing that he had learned something new from the experience.

These days we chat on the phone. The boys write good letters, and I am relieved that both can now read handwriting, for printing was never a talent of mine. Young Woo's family has given us so much joy and made our lives complete. We look forward to seeing more of Won Sook and Young Soo and their families.

We did not in any way finance Young Woo's coming to the United States nor his years at the University of Pittsburgh, since we were retiring and still had his sister in junior college and his brother in high school. Because social status in Korea was largely based on education, almost to the point of segregation, we strongly felt we had to help Won Sook and Young Soo complete their educations. A person lacking a high school diploma would be degraded, even by one's own family. Thus, we felt we must help if the family was to remain united.

Young Woo has many times expressed his appreciation that through our help all three siblings have successful lives. Won Sook became a librarian at Seoul Theological Seminary upon graduation from junior college. She married a young electrical engineer whom she met in her church choir. They and their two children lived in East Chicago, Indiana, while he completed his master's degree and did student teaching. He returned to a teaching position at Taegu University in Korea and plans to return to the United States in a few years to work on his doctorate. They visited us on their way home.

Young Soo, the brother, is the middle child, who was left to make his own way at age thirteen, when his mother died. He worked in a store long, merciless hours, getting his education at night school. Remembering how heavy my eyelids felt in night classes, I wondered how a growing boy, overworked and underfed, could keep awake, much less learn. At sixteen Young Soo enlisted in the Korean Marines and went to Vietnam at seventeen. He hoped to save money that would enable him to go to high school without having to work. Unfortunately, upon his return, he discovered that the military service plus overage excluded him from daytime high school classes. He was able, though, to combine night classes with day classes at the Institute and complete the requirements for his diploma. He is now the manager of a small jewelry shop. When Young Woo came to the United States, he turned the house in Seoul over to his brother, who lives there with his wife and three daughters.

Young Woo has wanted to repay us. He especially has wanted to pay our way to visit Korea. We know we have been repaid many times and rejoice that he is passing on whatever help we have given him to others that they, too, might have a better life.

A
Light in My Heart

1

Three Battles

I WAS NOT BORN BLIND. For the first fourteen years of my life, I could see normally. As I sit here typing, I can picture all the keys of the typewriter, my chair facing it, the door behind me, the hall, the closet door. I have a memory bank full of fourteen years of visual imagery.

I can visualize my past. I have retained the image of my birthplace—the small village near Seoul on the River Han—and scenes of my childhood. I can see my father, a farmer who owned a fleet of boats carrying produce back and forth to Seoul. In those days, life was placid and promising. As the second child, first son in an Asian household, I was especially favored by my parents. Mother taught me Bible stories and dreamed that I would become a minister in the family's Presbyterian faith. Father hoped I would grow up to be a lawyer.

Three months after I entered first grade, in June of 1950, war engulfed our peaceful village. North Korean divisions, armed and advised by the Soviet Union, launched a full-scale armored attack south across the thirty-eighth parallel, which had divided Korea since the end of World War II. Before we could flee, our village was occupied by communist troops. My family and others took refuge in the town hall.

United Nations forces struck back—first with air power and then by land and sea. Seoul was retaken in September, lost again in January, retaken in the spring. War swept back and forth across our village many times. Sometimes the Communists from the north were Korean, sometimes Chinese. Modern war is remote and implacably swift; it cannot differentiate between the enemy and the innocent. I saw some of my six-year-old friends and others die after getting shot. We did not know from where the bullets came. We could not even tell whether they were communist or "friendly"—we knew only that they were deadly. When the planes came—sometimes propeller-driven fighters, sometimes the new silvery jets—we shook our handkerchiefs to indicate we were civilians. I do not know whether or not it helped, but it was all we could do to protect ourselves.

One day our entire village was destroyed, and I saw the houses burning. Our house was burned and all our family possessions lost. We did not know how the fires began or who started them. I do know that after that the children were so hungry we tried to suck sap from trees.

After the peace talks at Panmunjom and the signing of an uneasy truce which stopped the fighting, my father decided to sell his land and move our family to Seoul. He managed to find work in the national tobacco industry. Today I remember my father as a man who struggled and sacrificed for his family. Although his spirit was wounded and drained of energy, his strength endured for five years. Then in 1957, he died. At age thirteen I had lost my home, my way of life, and my father. The following year began a new kind of terror and an even greater battle for me.

One day in the spring of 1958, while I was playing soccer with some school friends, a hard-kicked ball hit me in the left eye, and I reeled in pain and dizziness. In a short time the pain and the dizziness subsided, and life went on much as it had before. But then my vision began to dim, and I began to see a mixture of very small blind spots and bright sparks. Fearfully, my mother and I went from doctor to doctor, from hospital to hospital—searching for an answer, searching for a treatment, searching for hope.

I was nearsighted. At school, if I did not wear glasses, I had to sit in the front row to see what was written on the blackboard. In the United States, it is widely accepted that a high degree of nearsightedness is a major cause of retinal detachment. Eye specialists advise people with severe myopia to avoid contact sports like soccer. Seeing small blind spots and sparks is a major clinical symptom of retinal detachment. I was giving eye physicians perfect clinical clues, but it took five months of visits before the sixth eye specialist, who practiced at Severance Hospital, diagnosed the retinal detachment. The prognosis was gradual loss of vision leading to total blindness, unless the retina could be reattached.

The doctor said he could operate, but it was a very expensive procedure, and he was not overly optimistic. He said if the operation should fail, I should go to a school for the blind. I appreciated his truthfulness, but his pessimism, coupled with the fact that we were not able to pay for the costly surgery, scared us away.

A few months later, we learned physicians from developed countries were contributing services at Korea's National Medical Center. I was examined and began treatment there as an outpatient. Still, I had to wait several agonizing months before I was admitted as an inpatient on August 5, 1959, more than a year after the fateful accident.

The National Medical Center was originally built and operated by Denmark, Norway, and Sweden. Denmark's Dr. Larson, who chaired the eye department, prescribed complete bed rest for me. The hope was that the retinas would reattach spontaneously if there was absolutely no eye movement for several months. I spent eighty-eight days lying immobile with bandages over both eyes. Nurses fed me, bathed me, aided my every natural function. It was absolutely imperative that I not turn even my head. You cannot imagine how difficult, how actually painful it is for a healthy, active teenager to lie immobile for hours, days, weeks, months. Nothing could have inspired me to overcome such torture except the hope of restoring my sight.

Dr. Larson and his associates visited the ward daily. During each visit, he removed my bandages for a very short period of time. I could not identify my progress during the daily visits, but I felt there was overall improvement when my bandages were taken off on the eighty-eighth day.

Dr. Larson felt the bed rest treatment had failed. He ordered me to get up and walk. When I stepped down from the bed, my feet were swollen and hurt when I stood. Gradually, as nurses helped me learn to walk again, the pain disappeared, but as soon as I began to walk, my vision grew worse.

To understand retinal detachment, picture the retina of your eye as wallpaper on a wall of microscopic blood vessels. Detachment means the wallpaper is peeling off. It is not just a matter of putting the wallpaper back, because as it peeled away, it was cut off from the nourishment of the blood vessels, and parts of the retina die. Those parts cannot be revived.

When Dr. Larson first examined my eyes, he said it might be too late but he would do his best. Bed rest had been an attempt to save the remaining retinal tissue. When my vision worsened as I started walking, it was obvious the detachment was progressing. Vision by that time was failing fastest in my left eye, which was given up for lost. In hopes of saving the right eye, Dr. Larson elected to operate.

When the head nurse translated his decision into Korean for me, I was overjoyed. I had unquestioning faith—based solely on desperate hope—that the eye operation would bring my eyesight back. Every day of my bed rest I had asked the doctor, "When will you operate on my eyes?" I thought I would rather die on an operating table than be blind. At least an operation would mean that every avenue had been explored.

Early one morning, my hospital bed was moved toward the operating room. On the way it was stopped while many doctors shone lights into my eyes, drawing pictures on a large chart, talking and talking. Preparation for the surgery was extraordinarily meticulous, but finally the examinations ended. I asked a nurse for the time—it was 1:20 P.M. I was consumed by expectation, fear, and distress. I had missed three meals, but I did not feel hungry.

When I arrived in the operating room, a doctor said softly, "Take a deep breath." I fell instantly into deep sleep. I remember nothing of the operation, but I do remember waking gradually, hearing someone asking for "water . . . water." The someone, it turned out, was me. I was very thirsty.

Dr. Bon Sool Koo said, "You are waking."

"Please give me water—a glass of water," I said.

"If you drink water," the doctor said, "you will vomit. You have to wait."

Suddenly I forgot my thirst. I was overcome by a hopeless sense of disappointment and grief. The black spots and sparks were still moving under my closed eyelids. No one really had to tell me the operation had failed, but I could not quit hoping. I thought perhaps some sort of miracle would occur.

Dr. Larson gave me the harsh facts within a very few days. When my eyes had recovered sufficiently to be tested, the doctor carefully removed the bandages and addressed me in Korean.

"Can you see well?"

I looked around the room. "The operation did not make my vision better, but worse," I said. "I can see only forms and figures of the people around."

Dr. Larson and his staff were intensely disappointed. They were my friends and grieved for me. He said he would try again but would have to wait several months while I gained strength. I was fifteen years old, but after the first operation I weighed only seventy pounds, and disappointment had crippled my spirit.

My parents had emphasized religion in our home. Thus, every night I sat up in bed and prayed to stay in the world of light. When the second operation was about to be performed in the spring of

1960, I prayed even harder. I fantasized that when I awoke after the operation, I could see a little better; next day, still better; another day, better yet!

When the day of the operation finally came, I was so weak, doctors were reluctant to anesthetize my entire body. They decided to use a local anesthetic in my left eye. The pain of the injection is hard to describe, strange and excruciating. As the hours-long operation proceeded, the pain persisted and escalated, despite the anesthetic. When I could tolerate it no longer, I became violent. Doctors and nurses strapped my legs and my arms so that I could not move.

Again I prayed. I could do nothing else. I prayed, "Oh, Lord, I am willing to tolerate this hellish pain if it is given to me as the cost of regaining my sight. Sight will enable me to do greater things for the betterment of society."

At last Dr. Larson said, "I have finished."

All through the painful hours of surgery, I had waited for the moment when the black spots and bright sparks would disappear. To my dismay, I could still see them.

Two months later, Dr. Larson returned to Denmark; Dr. Koo became chairman of the eye department and took responsibility for my treatment. One Sunday night in July of 1960, Dr. Koo asked me to come to the inpatient doctor's office, only two doors east of my room, but to which I had never before been summoned. I went with misgiving.

When I sat down, Dr. Koo asked, "Who told you that your sight will never return?"

"No one," I replied.

"Then what has made you so moody and depressed?"

"In the three months since the second operation, my vision has become worse, and I see more sparks and strange spots in my eyes. That tells me that I will live in darkness. I do not want to become blind. Please do anything you can to restore my sight."

Dr. Koo did not hide the facts. "Your retina has totally

disintegrated," he said. "Even in the developed countries, modern eye specialists would not have been able to repair the damage. I suggest you seek rehabilitation to enable you to be self-functioning."

Although I had known I was going blind, I was shocked and terrified when the irrevocable facts were confirmed by the doctor, a distinguished authority in ophthalmological medicine.

That night, Dr. Koo told me the success stories of several blind people, among them that of Takeyo Ewahashi. Ewahashi was blinded when he was a student at Waseda University in Japan. As a blind person he went to England to do his graduate work and became a member of the faculty at Waseda when he returned to Japan. He pioneered in the field of blind rehabilitation by founding the Libon Light House for the Blind in Osaka. In my shock and despair, I was not impressed. When Dr. Koo suggested I might be able to become such a successful person, my reaction was anger! He and the hospital social worker, Miss Sun Hee Lee, tried to tell me that I could fight for a more useful life. However, I furiously rejected their attempts to help and turned to faith healing.

I heard of a young Pentecostal preacher who was reputed to have performed many miracles of healing and began attending his church. For two years, my brother guided me to services every Wednesday, Friday, and Sunday.

My first exposure to that church was a shock. The preacher was very young, and the congregation was so poor it worshiped in a large tent without chairs—worshipers sat on straw boxes. Many in the congregation were handicapped or seriously ill.

When I began attending, Dr. Cho had about five hundred parishioners. He spent a great deal of time praying for me and seemed to sincerely believe that God would restore my vision. I told him about my years of treatment with ophthalmologists, my months in the hospital, my eye surgery. When he prayed for me individually, he placed his hands over my eyes. He said devils were in my eyes. "I am ordering you, in the name of Jesus: release this man! Get out of here, bad evil!"

I waited for the sparks and spots to go away, but they did not. Oh, how I hoped they would disappear. I forced my faith, praying wholeheartedly that my vision be restored. I believed God could lift away the darkness.

"O Lord," Dr. Cho prayed, "be glorified by healing this person's eye condition, which cannot be treated by modern medicine." After he prayed hard and long, Dr. Cho would say, "God has now healed your eyes!" And he would ask me, "Can you see well now?"

I was embarrassed when he removed his hands from my eyes because I knew God had not restored my sight. The sparks and spots were still moving around as I moved my eyes, and my vision did not improve; indeed, gradually it grew worse.

In the depths of my despair, I thought, "Even God may not be able to give life again to the detached retina, to the irreplaceable tissue that has peeled away from my eye and died." Psychologically I suffered terribly; I began to think my eyesight was not being restored because I lacked faith in God, and the idea that either God had left me or I had left God was a terrible thing.

While I sought the restoration of sight through faith healing, we had slowly used up the remaining family savings that had come from the sale of our small farm. Finally I asked Dr. Cho whether I should give up perpetual prayer and seek a new life as a blind person. Reluctantly he said, "Yes."

*　*　*

Hospital visiting hours were from 1 to 2 P.M. on Tuesday, Thursday, and Saturday and from 1 to 3 P.M. on Sunday. My mother had visited me that fateful Sunday before Dr. Koo talked so frankly to me. I had to wait until Tuesday before I could share the burden of my bad news.

My mother came into the fading light of the hospital room

Tuesday afternoon. She doubtless was seeking for herself some assurance that her elder son would see again. She needed me to take my father's place in the family. Instead, I poured upon her my personal misery. When I reflect back to that day, I realize how saturated with grief my mother's heart must have been. It could absorb no more. She left the hospital in darkness, in the grip of the same terrible hopelessness that tore at her son. On the way, she stopped to see Dr. Koo, who confirmed the bleak prognosis.

She walked alone down the street toward our house, a house shorn of meaning without husband or elder son. Perhaps her last thoughts were of her son and his blindness. She died of a stroke eight hours after she left my hospital room.

Her death was kept from me during my remaining four months in the hospital. My sisters and brother told me that mother had hurt her leg and could not make the trip to the hospital. The fiction could be sustained because we did not have a telephone at home; in Korea in those days only the very rich had their own phones. In November, when I was released from the hospital, the truth could no longer be hidden.

I reacted, of course, with great grief, which turned to overpowering shame and guilt. I felt I was being punished by God. I felt guilty because I could not take my father's place as man of the house when he died. I felt guilty because I had not been stronger around my mother, done more to comfort her. Compounding the shame and the guilt was hopelessness and a profound sense of isolation. My despair was a terrible thing. Like Job in the Old Testament, I asked why God had allowed such misfortunes to be visited upon me.

Won Ja, my older sister, was seventeen when our mother died. She had to discontinue her high school studies and take on the responsibility of supporting me, my brother, and my younger sister. She worked as a tailor from 6 A.M. until 10 P.M. Eventually she became ill, refused all medical help, and died. She felt this world had asked more of her than she could bear. She did not care if she left it. She had lost her will to live.

Won Ja's death came just sixteen months after our mother's stroke. In four short years, I had lost my home, my father, my eyesight, my mother, and my older sister. I felt totally alone and felt that even God, whom I had loved and trusted, had abandoned me. All my strength was gone.

In Korea, blind people were viewed with fright and superstition. Some persons—particularly the uneducated—spit at blind people on the streets, saying "No luck today!" Worse, Korea lacked welfare or rehabilitation programs for the handicapped. In that environment, there was no hope. I could not even imagine a professional career. I knew the only occupations open to people without sight were fortune-telling and massage. My brother was thirteen years old and my sister was nine. They were my responsibility, but I could think of no way to support them. I cried and cried with them.

"I would be able to support you if I were not blind," I said.

Again I considered suicide, but I had already learned that committing suicide is as difficult as survival for a blind person. During my hospital stay, I collected sleeping pills and painkillers by complaining of headaches and sleeplessness. One day I thought I had enough to kill myself. At midnight, I swallowed them all. When I regained consciousness, I learned that I had accidentally touched the call-bell. A nurse responded, discovered what I had done, and called the doctor. God did not want me to find peace through death. I have never seriously considered suicide since then.

Instead, I decided to seek a new life.

2

Beginning a New Life

ONE MONTH BEFORE I was discharged, the hospital social worker, Miss Sun Hee Lee, visited me in my room to once again encourage me to enter a school for the blind. I would not hear of it. I was angry. "I can take care of myself after I'm discharged," I said. "Please leave me alone. I will never go to the school for the blind. I am not blind. My vision will improve."

She left the room without saying more.

After the two years in Dr. Cho's church and having given up on faith healing, I remembered her offer of help. I could no longer deny the fact that I was legally blind and that even my faint remaining sight was fading. Somehow I rallied the courage to see if her offer still stood.

I was not sure that she was still the resident social worker, but when I went to the hospital and knocked on the door that led to her office, I found she was, indeed, still there. She was surprised to see me, but she made me welcome. "Yesterday," said Miss Lee, "I saw Dr. Koo in the corridor. He asked about you. It is really a remarkable coincidence that you are visiting today."

The obstacles to immediate rehabilitation were staggering. Our family savings were used up. The three of us—my brother, my sister, and me—could not support ourselves. I told Miss Lee that my brother, then thirteen years old, had a job at a hardware store during the day and studied at night school, but my sister, who was nine, could not work. I asked Miss Lee if she could be placed in an orphanage so that I could go to a boarding school for the blind.

Another social worker overheard our conversation and arranged for the placement of my sister, Won Sook, in Seoul's Hemyung Orphanage, which was operated by Buddhists and supported by the Canadian Unitarian Service. The arrangement permitted Won Sook to continue her education, and in that I was happy.

When the day came that we had to go our separate ways, the three of us cried and cried. We knew, though, that it was the best arrangement at that time.

Miss Lee helped me to receive basic training for a month at the Rehabilitation Center for the Blind of Korea. As modest as the tuition was, I could not afford to pay even that small amount. Miss Lee arranged it for me, and I began the training in January 1962. The rehabilitation center was a small private agency, the only one of its kind in Korea at that time. Founded and operated by Dr. Byung Woo Kong, the first Korean ophthalmologist, it received neither government subsidy nor private contributions but was funded solely through Dr. Kong's humanitarian philanthropy.

Dr. Kong, incidentally, is the father of the Korean typewriter—the "Hangeul" typewriter. As an outstanding ophthalmologist, he agonized over the helplessness of patients who were going blind. On a visit to the United States in the nineteen-fifties, he saw that blind Americans could communicate using typewriters. As soon as he returned to Korea he developed a research institute to produce a compact Korean typewriter, and he established the rehabilitation center to give practical training to the blind as well as to give hope.

When I attended Dr. Kong's center, one sighted administrator, one blind teacher, and eight newly-blind people were there. On my first day, I learned that the blind teacher worked at the center during the day, then studied at Keonkook University at night. It was the first time I realized a blind person could go to college. I was tremendously impressed, and a new seed of hope was planted.

During my month at the rehabilitation center, I learned to use the Hangeul typewriter and to write Braille. Reading Braille is much more difficult than writing it, and I did not learn to read it until long after I left the center. My sense of touch was not yet sharp enough, perhaps, but to be honest, I did not work that hard at Braille. I practiced typing much more conscientiously, and I felt very rewarded by the fact that I was one of very few Koreans who could type at that time. I identified more with the sighted than with the blind, and I especially wanted to communicate with sighted people, particularly the doctors and nurses who cared for me.

Braille is named for Louis Braille, a blind Frenchman who introduced the basic system in the nineteenth century. Braille is actually an adaptation of a tactile alphabet developed by a French army officer so that military messages could be read in the dark. Louis Braille substituted raised dots for raised letters. The system was not universally adopted immediately, however. Considerable debate was held about whether it or subsequently developed systems of raised dots were best, but by 1932, Standard English Braille was established as the standard code of tactile communication for blind persons. Establishment of a standard made it possible for all Braille readers to read all Braille writing no matter who trained them, or where.

The basic unit of Braille is a quadrangular "cell" containing from one to six dots. The different "dialects" of Braille vary primarily in the number of contractions used. For example, Grade 1 Braille contains no contractions; Grade 2 Braille makes considerable use of contractions and shortened forms of words.

One may write Braille in two ways—the Braille typewriter and the slate-and-stylus. The "Brailler" has six keys, one for each of the six dots of the cell. A combination of the keys, when depressed simultaneously, leaves a unique embossed print on paper. The slate-and-stylus is more portable than the typewriter but more difficult to use. The stylus must be pressed through the openings of the slate, which sandwiches paper between its two halves. The slate-and-stylus is also slower. The stylus makes an indentation in the paper, so the Braille cells have to be written in reverse order.

The Korean Braille system is based on the same six dots. Music and mathematics and scientific notation are all depicted by different combinations of the dots, but there is an awkward overlap. For example, dot 1 is the letter *a* in English; it is another letter in Korean; it means something else in music.

As I practiced Braille writing and reading, I experienced a new wave of frustration and disappointment. It was becoming increasingly clear to me that everything in the world of the blind was cumbersome and slow. The sighted can do sums on any old piece of paper. The blind require a metal slate with lead type; they practically have to hand-set each figure. When I had my sight, I could pick up a pencil and write anything anywhere. Blind, I had to use ungainly equipment. Worse, what used to take me a few hours to read now took me weeks. I used to hear of a book and get it from a library or bookstore—suddenly I had to order it from abroad. Often it would not be available in Braille. I used to use a pocket dictionary. The same dictionary takes twenty huge Braille volumes.

The many disadvantages curbed my enthusiasm for Braille, but I was exceptionally motivated to learn typing. If I could type, I could correspond with sighted friends and relatives. Before going to the rehabilitation center, I did not even imagine that I would ever again be able to write to the sighted.

Dr. Koo was the first to encourage me to seek rehabilitation. My first letter was to him and expressed my sincere appreciation for his concern and compassion. Impressed, he replied quickly, ". . . Your typed letter was so inspirational that I took the liberty of showing it to the doctors and nurses who are still interested in you."

On that day when Dr. Koo told me about Takeyo Ewahashi, a Japanese professor who took his graduate studies at Edinburgh University in Britain, I saw little relationship between me and such a success story. But there in the rehabilitation center in Seoul I typed another letter in quick reply to the doctor: "I believe that Mr. Ewahashi can serve as my model. He has shown what a blind person can do to better society. I will become a Korean Ewahashi."

More than twenty years have passed since Dr. Koo and I began to exchange letters. Those first two letters were instrumental in developing a real friendship between a distinguished physician and a struggling patient. In the ensuing decades, Dr. Koo has affected my life in every way—directly and indirectly—as one of my major benefactors.

Dr. Kong often visited the students at his rehabilitation center. He joined in our recreational activities and even ate meals that had been prepared by the students, an unusual occurrence in Korea. Dr. Kong treated us with dignity. At that time, I suffered from feelings of inferiority, a lack of confidence, an inadequate concept of self, and no fighting spirit. Dr. Kong's attitudes began to shape my own. He influenced me to look beyond blindness, to regain self-worth and human dignity.

After mastering basic rehabilitation skills—like typing and Braille writing—I was ready to enter the Seoul National School for the Blind. One day in March of 1962, three of us from the rehabilitation center were scheduled to take the entrance examination, and Dr. Kong arranged for us to go in his own car. It was my first experience riding in any car other than public bus or taxi. Our egos were further enlarged when we later learned that the doctor had used the car for his three blind protégés when his wife had wanted the car that day for a school affair involving one of their sons. How we enjoyed that special ride.

The center's blind teacher, Mr. Chun, was very mobile. With a cane, he traveled safely and independently even in downtown Seoul. He was mobile enough to mingle with sighted people. One day Mr. Chun asked me if I would like to attend weekly Quaker meetings with him. On Sunday I did not have anything special to do, and I was curious to find out how a blind man could mingle with the sighted at the meeting. I agreed to go. Mr. Chun led me confidently and safely, and we neither fell into a pit nor bumped into anything.

The Quakers were a small group. They all knew each other, and they seemed free from the usual Korean prejudice against blind people. I felt very welcome. Because of that acceptance, I attended many weekly Quaker meetings and made many friends. Dr. Kong, incidentally, also attended the Quaker meetings. In fact, it was he who provided the meeting place.

This transitional period at the rehabilitation center, though very brief, had been happy and rewarding. When the time came to leave, I felt sad and reluctant.

Miss Lee arranged to pay my entrance fee and tuition for the first three months at the Seoul School for the Blind. She guided me to a shopping center nearby so that we could get items necessary for my new dormitory life. It must have been embarrassing for her as a young Korean woman to be seen guiding me in the marketplace. Some merchants, vying for her attention, called her "Auntie." I was embarrassed for her, but Miss Lee did not seem to mind, and her help was invaluable.

Finally my new life began at the school for the blind. Unlike the hospital or the rehabilitation center, I ran into many adjustment problems. I worried about the future—the short-term future. The school was run by the Korean government, but students had to pay tuition nonetheless. Miss Lee had taken care of the first three months' tuition, but I had no idea from where subsequent funds would come.

The food was terrible. I could not get used to the meals provided at school. I skipped so many meals that I used to get so hungry I would actually suffer hunger pains. I hated the taste and smell of the food and did not think about the lack of nutrition. I envied my fellow students who could afford to eat out when they liked or who could go home over a weekend or during vacation. I had little remaining vision by that time, but with that little I looked for magic stars in the sky and prayed fervently for money enough to buy good food.

To make matters worse, I was in deep trouble the first week because I inadvertently broke one of the rules. In the school for the blind, as well as throughout Korea, juniors respect and obey their seniors. It is an unbreakable rule, and the principle is even incorporated in the Korean language. Verb endings in Korean are different for elders and superiors than for juniors or subordinates.

I had completed eight years of school before I began to lose my sight, but I lost two years while I was hospitalized. At the school for the blind I had to go back to the seventh grade to take up the curriculum leading to the only available vocational education—basic medical science, massage, and acupuncture. Thus, I was older and larger than most of my classmates.

One day that first week I saw—I could still see dim shapes—a small student walking ahead of me. "Where," I asked, "do you buy the thick Braille paper?" Assuming he was my junior, I did not use the respectful verb form.

A very strict eleventh grade student whipped me with a broom until my hip was swollen and bleeding. I was furious. I could not understand how he could be so brutal to one of his blind classmates. I discussed the incident with Miss Lee, and she protested for me. The dormitory manager forced the eleventh grader to apologize to me, and the matter was closed, but I have never forgotten that experience.

The only occupation open to me after graduation, I was told, was that of masseur. Once more I sank into despair. I heard some fellow students say, "I would rather be a soothsayer and make more money right now!" Later I learned that they left the school.

I felt that that door was closed to me. Both my mother and father were active Christians and church officers. They enjoyed

serving ministers visiting the church and risked their lives
sheltering pastors during the war. My mother dreamed that I
would become a Christian minister. If I had even considered the
possibility of becoming a fortune-teller, she would have cried in
heaven.

In those days, blind Korean masseurs were identified by the
sound of their bamboo clarinet which they played as they moved
about the streets. When a customer heard the sound, he would call
out. It was a depressing, sad sound, and it made me ashamed and
embarrassed because of the pity and sympathy it elicited from
sighted people. I hated the sound and the pity. Remarkably, I had
adjusted to the point that I felt challenged to find another suitable
occupation.

Like most sighted people, I believed then that the blind have a
sixth sense—greater memory or more capacity for concentration.
Some of my classmates seemed that way, but I could not even read
Braille. It was many months before I could study Braille texts on
my own, so I evolved a system, allowing me to obtain information
from Braille texts even though I could not yet read them. Some of
the students needed tutorial or remedial instruction. I offered to
help. I would act as their tutor; they would read the Braille text.
They appreciated my help and did not know they were also helping
me. I continued to help classmates who needed it even after
acquiring enough skill in reading Braille to study on my own. It
was really my first experience with teaching.

Later, of course, I learned that the blind have no special senses;
they simply make better use of the senses they have. That
enhancement peaks, perhaps, in the phenomenon known as
"facial vision"—an ability to sense obstacles and terrain by sound
and the feel of the air around them. The air at the edge of a roof
feels lighter than the air near a table. Sounds echo differently
depending on the size and content of a room. Air in the middle of
the block feels different than the air at a street corner. Facial vision
can be developed to the point that—if there are no distracting

sounds—you can tell a wall from a tree, a tree from a lamppost, a lamppost from a mailbox. You will not know exactly what they are, but you will know they have different bulk, and you will make the appropriate surmises.

Those who lose their sight in early childhood are able to sharpen facial vision naturally and fearlessly, but people like me who lose sight after several years are less likely to develop the same degree of ability. Most of my classmates had more mobility than I, and they read and wrote Braille more quickly. I felt inferior and frustrated until I realized that the majority of them had not been able to see since they were very young.

In South Korea, there are thirteen schools for the blind. All of them require that a sightless child stay night and day, seeing parents only on weekends and vacation. Blind children are not "mainstreamed"—they are not sent to school with those who can see. Yet the integration of blind and sighted children in classrooms was tried very early in Korea, about 1900. Dr. Rosetta Sherwood Hall, a Methodist missionary physician, placed two blind girls in classes with sighted students at Jungjin in Elementary School in Pyongyang, North Korea. She believed that integrated education could better foster self-reliance and self-esteem in the blind children. Unfortunately, the experiment came to an end after Japanese occupation in 1910. I favor integrated day schools, and I sincerely hope blind Korean children can experience main-streaming, but I do not deny that the residential school has its own advantages. The Seoul School for the Blind gave me one incomparable experience. I was an equal, totally accepted, treated like everyone else. Being blind did not make me special. I did not have to cope with the negative attitudes of others.

3

Dreams Come True

I HAD A DREAM to go to college, but I had no means of achieving this goal since all my material resources were gone. It seemed hopeless. Slowly, however, I began to feel that God, working through angels in the guise of human beings, was revealing a purpose for my life, that the pain and suffering would be rewarded with a plan for making my dream come true.

At one of the Quaker meetings, I met Miss Soon Kwi Kwon, a Girl Scout troop leader. When she learned of my plight, she initiated a fund drive among members of her troop. That initial fund paid for three months of my school expenses, and when that was gone Miss Kwon paid my tuition for one year from her own purse. She visited me at school once a month to give me the monthly check. She never mailed it. When she was too busy to come, she invited me to visit her. Thus we saw each other regularly.

As a representative of Korea's Quakers, Miss Kwon attended an international conference in Pakistan. When she returned, she brought me a harmonica as a present, and it was a friend for a long time. When my roommates went home over the weekend and I was alone, it was a source of comfort and joy.

One day in March of 1963, Miss Kwon visited me as usual, but she was depressed, and her voice was deeply troubled. "Unfortunately," she said, "one of my brothers has been laid off. I can no longer afford to support your schooling. I must pay my nephew's tuition instead."

I felt my only source of help was gone, but I learned quickly that God had closed one door only to open another. I learned from a surprise letter that the hospital social worker who had been so instrumental in getting me to try rehabilitation was receiving professional training in the United States.

"I am very pleased," Miss Lee wrote, "to introduce a kind American couple who are willing to underwrite your education. I sincerely hope that you will become a model and guide for those handicapped persons who are unfortunate like yourself. I am confident that you can make it with your fine intellect and strong determination."

Within a few months, I received another letter—this one from Mr. and Mrs. Frazier McNeill, who had no children of their own. They were sincere Christians. They had helped an engineering student from Iran and were financially assisting a nephew. Mr. McNeill was a pioneer of Goodwill Industries, a social and rehabilitation service agency for the disabled, and a dedicated Rotarian. Mrs. McNeill was a junior high school financial manager. They paid my tuition and living expenses for nine years until I graduated from Yonsei University. We exchanged letters every other week. I felt as close to them as to my natural parents.

The McNeills eliminated my financial worry, but I was still plagued by inner conflict. I could not shake the idea that I was being punished for something: God did not heal my eye disease because I did not believe strongly enough. The conflict was magnified because my desperate turn to faith healing had not been successful.

One Sunday evening in 1964 I happened to hear a program called "Life Counseling" on the Christian Broadcasting System. When the announcer mentioned the counselor, Rev. Byung Sub Van, I was very pleased because I recognized the name. Rev. Van had visited our hometown church and often had been a visitor in our home. It had been about ten years since I had seen him last.

I typed a letter to Rev. Van, telling him of my spiritual conflict. At that time I had even stopped going to church, thinking the God I had trusted had abandoned me. Rev. Van replied immediately. He asked me to meet him at the CBS office the following Tuesday afternoon, where he addressed my innermost feelings. "Suffering has a purpose," he said. God eventually makes that purpose clear through an individual's experiences. Sometimes God heals a physical disability, sometimes he does not. If he does not, he gives the sufferer the power to bear it. Rev. Van quoted John 9:1–3, "As he passed by, he saw a man blind from his birth. And his disciples asked him, 'Rabbi, who sinned, this man or his parents, that he was born blind?' Jesus answered, 'It was not that this man sinned, or his parents, but that the works of God might be made manifest in him.' "

I was also reminded that the Apostle Paul asked God three times to heal the thorn in his flesh. God did not heal Paul. Instead he answered, "My grace is sufficient for you, for my power is made perfect in weakness" (2 Cor. 12:9).

As I thought of Paul, I felt an exhilarating sense of identity with him. As with the Apostle, God's truth came to me in a flash of inner vision, and a great burden of guilt was lifted from my soul. With my guilt and anxiety quelled, I was free to devote most of my time and energies to studies, even to plan a professional career that went beyond massage and acupuncture.

Rev. Van's counseling program broadcast my story. From the radio audience came a unique response: one young Christian man offered to donate one of his eyes to me. He said he could function with a single eye, and I would be able to do more with the donated eye than he ever could. The young man was deeply disappointed when he was informed that entire eye transplants were not possible, that only a cornea could be transplanted, and I did not need a cornea. We became friends, that young man and I, and it turned out that he had two brothers living in the Los Angeles area who met the McNeills, my American parents.

Convinced at last that God had a plan for my life, I grew even more determined to master my handicap. My first challenge was to win middle school and high school diplomas by passing examinations.

My sighted peers were already in high school. I was four years older than my classmates. That did not make a great deal of difference at the school for the blind because many of the students, for a variety of reasons, were older, but I wanted, inordinately, to be in the same grade with my sighted friends.

In order to skip some grades and catch up, I decided to attend a special educational institute for poor students who could not afford to go to regular schools. I could go at night, studying by day at the school for the blind. I did just that for three months, but it proved difficult. I could not leave the dormitory at night if there were student council or dormitory activities. I was absent too many times, but I went on doggedly, feeling I had to be in the same grade as my friends.

One night during the third month of my educational "shortcut," I fell into a pit left by road construction workers. I had never had proper orientation and mobility training, as such training did not then exist in Korea. Water was in the pit, causing me to scramble out quickly. I had a pain in the area of my left ribs, but X rays showed no damage. The embarrassing misstep convinced me, however, that I was courting disaster, perhaps even further disability. Thus, I gave up the "shortcut."

More than one-third of the subjects at the school for the blind dealt with basic medical science, massage, acupuncture, physical therapy. I was an honor student, but I knew that I would never be able, with that kind of educational background, to pass any university entrance examination. If I neglected the vocational subjects I could lose my honor student status. I could also be ostracized by the blind teachers, and I did not want that.

Therefore, I studied the vocational subjects along with the other subjects; I studied hard and did well and took part in student activities.

Before Korea was liberated from Japan, graduates of the school for the blind were certified to practice acupunture as well as massage. The first American-educated minister of Korea's Department of Health and Social Affairs changed the rules, however. Blind persons could no longer get a license to practice acupuncture. Ever since that rule, blind students have been fighting to turn the calendar back. When I was in school, the students went on a hunger strike, even staging a demonstration in front of the National Assembly building. I believed in their cause. I felt the right to practice acupuncture was essential to the ability of some blind persons to make a living. As a student leader, I took time to meet with some policymakers, going with the school principal and the president of the Korean Association of the Welfare of the Blind, to advocate certifying the blind to practice acupuncture. It was a losing battle. The right to practice acupuncture has never been regained.

My strategy for developing a professional career was to maintain an A average at the school and devote the rest of my time to college preparation. Fortunately some college student volunteers were available to me through the Red Cross.

*   *   *

On the third Sunday in May 1962, I met Kyoung Sook Suk. She was at a meeting of the Girl Scout troop that had raised funds for part of my tuition. Miss Kwon, the leader, had invited me to the meeting to cheer me up and to introduce her Girl Scouts to the blind man who had benefited from their money. When the meeting ended, Miss Kwon said, "You girls please wait here until I guide Young Woo to his bus stop." Kyoung volunteered to guide me. As we walked through heavy traffic, she asked many questions about my life at the school for the blind and what she could do for me. I was not at a loss for words. "I am hungry for knowledge. You can be my reader, if you do not mind."

Three weeks later Miss Kwon and Kyoung visited me at the dormitory. Every weekend thereafter, Kyoung visited me as a volunteer reader. Her interest expanded to encompass other blind students, and she learned a great deal about the unique needs of blind children. Active in the Red Cross and other service organizations, she recruited student volunteers to visit, read, and "work to make the blind more cheerful."

As the number of her visits increased, Kyoung and I began to develop a very special relationship. Then in 1963 we were separated for many weeks. Unlike the United States, Korean schools and colleges have long winter vacations. Kyoung was a freshman at Sookmyung Women's University, a prestigious school. She spent her two-and-one-half months' winter vacation at the home of her parents in Kunsan. I missed her, and she must have missed me, too. One day in March I received a letter from Kyoung, and she wrote, "I am having a very nice time with my parents and old friends but miss our time at your school. I am very much looking forward to seeing you again in a week, as soon as the new academic year begins. I would like to do even more for you as your big sister from now on."

It was her decision. She neither consulted me nor asked my consent, but I confess I did not object. I never had reason to deny a wonderful opportunity to have a sister like her—a pretty, compassionate, and competent college student. Perhaps the decision came easily because she did not realize at the time that I was only one-and-a-half years younger than she. I must have looked much younger because I wore a middle-school uniform, required in those days, and there was a huge gap between the usual middle schooler and a college freshman.

At any rate, she returned to Seoul in a new role. She was not just my volunteer reader anymore; she was my big sister. In addition to reading, she began to take care of some of my daily needs. She washed my clothes, did some of my sewing, and went shopping with me.

Kyoung played a vital role in helping me prepare for the very competitive Yonsei University entrance examination. Every weekday night for several months, she walked me to the Korea Herald English Institute, meeting me at my bus stop and guiding me back to the bus after the lesson. She was impressed by the fact that I spoke English as well as most other college students at the Institute and better than some. Kyoung was vice-president of the Korean Red Cross College Student Association, and she recruited several of the students to tutor me in mathematics.

Kyoung's help, and that of her friends, was invaluable, but I was still anxious. I wanted to go to one of the best universities—like Yonsei—but I had no way of knowing whether I could pass the entrance examination. If you were a regular high school student, your teachers could compare each of the college and university admission standards with your achievement level and provide appropriate guidance. The school for the blind offered no such guidance.

One day in January 1967, I contacted the placement office of Seoul National University and arranged to hire a tutor for one year. A sophomore majoring in Korean language and literature was introduced to me. He turned out to be a very good tutor, and we became close friends. He evaluated my achievement level and assured me that I would be able to pass the entrance examination to a top university. I could not wait to spread that good news among my teachers and friends. Most of them laughed at my plan to go to Yonsei University. They said I could only count on being an applicant, not a student. "If you really want to go to college," they said, "you must choose a second-class university!"

Finally, in January of 1968, it was time to apply. Yonsei was one of the most prestigious institutions in Korea. It was sponsored by the Christian church (interdenominational), but it would not allow me to take the entrance examination. It held to the prevailing practice in most Korean colleges and universities: the handicapped were not permitted even to apply.

I protested loudly and strongly. I questioned how a Christian institution could discriminate so unjustly, so unreasonably. The protest came to naught. I walked away from the campus feeling totally rejected and helpless. At the bus stop, I told my sister, Won Sook, to get us on a bus going downtown. I was not totally without resources; I had one final card to play.

Rev. Kwon Suk Kim, general secretary of the National Council of Churches, had been sheltered in our home in the early days of the Korean War. He came from North Korea. I did not remember him because I was so young when he stayed with us; I knew of him through another wartime refugee, a seminary professor who had stayed with us much longer. I had visited her shortly after I was discharged from the hospital, and she suggested I also visit Rev. Kim. When I telephoned him, he remembered immediately the Kang home in Moonhori where he was sheltered. He was shocked to discover I was blind. "What happened to you?" he asked. I still remember the sadness in his voice.

Rev. Kim since then has gone out of his way to help and encourage me, acting when necessary as my guardian. Thus, after my application was rejected at Yonsei University, I went downtown on the bus with my sister to see Rev. Kim. He listened carefully to my story and told me to leave the application with him. Later I learned that Rev. Kim contacted the director of the university's general affairs department, who in turn contacted the Dean of the College of Liberal Arts, the Chairman of the Department of Education, and the Dean of Students. I was permitted to take the examination.

When I went for the first day of the tests, Professor Yu from the Department of English and English Literature was waiting for me. The room was empty except for the two of us. At times Dean Sung of the College of Liberal Arts and other concerned professors came into the room. Professor Yu read each of the questions. He wrote down my answers. I was allowed an extra half hour for each subject, and I knew I did well on the Korean language and English tests. On the second day, the additional thirty minutes were not granted, but no one had told me about the change. I expected more time, and I was embarrassed because I was sure I would need the extra time for the math test. Indeed, I did. The last test, history, was no problem. I did not need additional time for history. For two weeks I fretted, unnerved by the fact that I had not finished the math test. Then, at last, the results were announced.

I passed! Actually, I placed tenth among hundreds of applicants to the Department of Education. My performance could pave the way for other handicapped applicants.

I knew I had triumphed with God's help. I felt grateful to God for victory over all kinds of handicaps, and the thanks that I gave seemed more precious, somehow, than all the thanks that had gone before. Everyone who had said I could not go to a top university was wrong. My faith returned. God had a plan for my life all along, and all this time, instead of rejecting me, God had been revealing that plan through other people.

The McNeills, back in Los Angeles, had gone into their adoption of a blind Korean expecting to furnish $10 to $25 a month to see me through high school. No one had mentioned college. What would be their reaction? They replied that they would see me through college if I could be admitted.

4

Yonsei University:
Back to the World of the Sighted

WHEN I WAS IN HIGH SCHOOL, I had no idea what I should study in college in order to help other disabled people. At that time, no Korean college or university offered special education or rehabilitation programs. At first I planned to study clinical psychology. To do so, I would have to go to Korea University, as Yonsei had no department of psychology.

One day in October 1967, Dr. Perkins, Dean of California State College at Los Angeles and a friend of my American parents, visited me in Seoul. I talked with her about my planned curriculum and about the chances of continuing my education in the United States. She suggested that graduate work in the United States in the fields of rehabilitation counseling or special education would further my goals. She advised that I do my undergraduate work in education. She also promised to help me get into an American graduate school and to guide me in postgraduate study. Tragically, that was not to be. Dr. Perkins died within two years—a victim of cancer.

On the strength of her advice, I made my decision to apply to the Department of Education at Yonsei University. I chose Yonsei over Korea largely because it was Christian, founded by an American missionary, and enjoyed a fine reputation for teaching English. There was a saying that "even the dogs around Yonsei University campus bark in English!"

The two schools, both located in Seoul, have long been rivals on the academic and athletic fields. Both have produced distinguished national leaders in all fields, but it is the popular conception that Korea University carries on the Oriental tradition, and Yonsei University carries on the Western tradition.

The precept of Yonsei University is taken from John 8:32: "And you will know the truth, and the truth will set you free."

It was a difficult choice, but I have never regretted my decision—not even when Yonsei appeared to have rejected my application because of my blindness.

With the written exams passed, I was notified in February 1968 of the oral entrance examination. Four faculty members from the education department were waiting.

"Why," asked Dean Nae Woon Sung, "have you applied to Yonsei University's Department of Education?"

"Because," I said, "I would like to establish special education and rehabilitation programs at the college level in Korea. After receiving my B.A. degree from Yonsei, I plan to take graduate degrees in special education and rehabilitation in the United States."

The dean's reply was, really, a kind of benediction. "Helen Keller won her human victory with three disabilities," he said. "You *can* achieve you life goal with one disability."

It was the only question on the examination. The other three members of the oral examination team were tremendously supportive. Professor K. H. Oh said, "Your vision is so clear!" Professor C. S. Shim, "We have been waiting for a student like you who is so motivated to educate unfortunate, disabled persons." Professor R. S. Kim, "We really welcome you as our special student. We do hope you will enjoy your campus life. Please do not hesitate to seek our help when needs arise."

Entering Yonsei University not only enlarged my vision of the world, it enlarged my world's physical scale. Literally, it meant I had graduated into the world of the sighted from the world of the blind.

At the Seoul School for the Blind, the buildings were small, and corridors were barely wide enough for two persons to pass. We moved through the halls braced for collision, and if we bumped into someone, one of us stepped aside and fingered our way along the wall. We thought nothing of it. At Yonsei the walls seemed a mile apart. I could get lost trying to find the opposite wall. The large buildings were often separated by a mile or more.

The experience was traumatic for me and for my fellow students, who had never had a blind classmate. I hated to bump into people—especially females. While at the school for the blind it did not mean a thing, at the university it embarrassed others as well as me. Once in the right classroom, I had to learn to find my chair gracefully with a minimum of bumping. Students generally tried to be nice. They helped me from class to class, but they did not always know how. Some were too shy, and some were afraid I might be embarrassed.

In a few months, I made steady friends. They acted as my sighted guides throughout my undergraduate school life. One of those friends is Chang Kyu Ahn, who has developed a career as a mobility specialist. He did graduate work at Western Michigan University and teaches blind people how to travel safely and independently.

The new university life made me keenly aware of my blindness. It intensified my desire to read printed books. Moreover, it became essential that I find some way to read such books. Neither Braille nor talking texts were available, as they had been at the school for the blind, and reading assignments, as in colleges everywhere, were endless, continuing, demanding. I had to find a way to solve that very real, very urgent problem.

The concept of "volunteer reader" was totally new in Korea. Kyoung had been my reader, but during my freshman year at Yonsei, she was in the United States studying blind rehabilitation. I turned again to Dr. Koo, who secured a grant and established a small Braille library at his hospital. I had my foreign language texts

(English and German) translated into Braille, but that took care of only a portion of the problem.

My house near the campus was open to friends. When they stopped by, I taught them how to tape other textbooks. They did it at their convenience and enjoyed it. They were helping a friend. To add spice to the sauce, I shared with them my summaries of those tapes, and that helped them better prepare for their tests. As word of the two-way exchange made its way around the campus, I attracted enough volunteers to "read" all my texts.

Professors were another problem. They had never had a blind student. They did not seem to mind that I was in their classes, but they just did not know how to provide special help. I had to help them develop methods of giving me tests, for instance. Sometimes they read the questions; sometimes they relegated the task to teaching assistants.

One day in my sophomore year, I asked Professor Baek Sun Sung, instructor of educational psychology, how I should take the midterm. He gave it to me orally in his office, and I was particularly grateful for the time he spent with me. I studied hard, but when the results were announced, I was shocked to hear that I had an eighty—the lowest grade I had ever received. I could not believe it, and my disbelief increased when a few minutes later I heard that a student whom I had tutored had received a ninety-two. I began to suspect that some old Korean prejudices against the blind were clouding the issue. Since Professor Sung had tested me orally, there was no paper to check. I implored him to have his teaching assistant read the questions and record my answers. The professor agreed to accept that, and my score increased to ninety-eight.

After that, Professor Sung became deeply interested in my progress. At Christmas that year, I received a very special card from him. It said simply, "Go forward!" It meant much to me because a negative attitude had changed.

I took lecture notes in Braille and typed term papers on my Korean typewriter. There were occasional difficulties, but generally I felt I was doing very well. I made straight A's four semesters out of eight.

Physical education and military training are required in Korean general education. Since I could not meet those requirements as sighted students met them, I consulted the instructors. The military training instructor, a Yonsei University Theological Seminary graduate, was so understanding that he waived the physical aspects of the course. He required me, instead, to submit two term papers on anticommunism and mind training. I got A's in the course. The instructor of physical education said, "You do not need to attend the class. All you have to do is to submit a paper on physical education." I was grateful for his understanding. I did not dream the situation would turn into a nightmare. As directed, I did not attend class, and toward the end of the semester, I turned in my term paper. He gave me an F.

I still recall vividly—it was like the end of the world. My hopes of continuing to be a top student were dashed and I protested. Apparently he had not read my paper and had made no note of the reason for my absenteeism. He said, "In order to change your grade, I would have to make a written apology that might affect my job and my future." He promised he would process the term paper and regrade my performance if I would register again for physical training, but he would not publicly admit his mistake.

I did register and take the course again, but I made sure I had a different instructor. I could not afford another such disaster. The F lowered my grade point average just enough to keep me from becoming the highest honor student in the College of Liberal Arts, and I graduated with the second highest average.

I was very proud of being an education student at Yonsei. My self-esteem was enhanced, and I found new meaning to my life. A great deal of negativism existed in parts of the student body concerning my blindness. Some students openly said, "How embarrassing it is to have a blind person in our class!" My growing self-confidence and self-esteem helped me shrug off such thoughtlessness day to day. I was secure in my scholastic abilities, but I wanted to take part in extracurricular activities, and that turned out to be very difficult because of incipient student rejection.

I applied to a student circle called Heungsadan. Its purpose was to develop leadership through study of the thoughts of teacher Chang Ho Ahn, a noted Korean educator and leader. My application was rejected. Members of the circle tried to convince me that my blindness would make it difficult to participate in Heungsadan activities. They believed my blindness affected other human factors, that it circumscribed positive personality traits, independence, and psychological normalcy. These, remember, were not illiterate peasants; they were students in one of Korea's outstanding universities. I could not convince them that blindness means loss of eyesight—nothing more.

In the face of rejection, I persuaded a close friend to apply with me to another student circle. It was a club composed of education students from four different first-class universities, housed at the Seoul YMCA. I convinced myself this distinguished, homogeneous group had outgrown Korea's medieval attitude toward blindness, that its Christian members would show Christian compassion. I was sure they would accept me in order to have my very popular friend, but my friend's application was rejected along with mine.

I was furious and frustrated, but I did not think of giving up. I could not surrender to unjust discrimination, to unthinking negative prejudice. Fighting mad, I was determined to found an ideal student circle.

At first, I tried to organize an academic circle composed of education and psychology students. Speaker at the first meeting was Professor Sung Tae Kim of Korea University, the educator who had obtained permission for me to take entrance examinations there before I decided to attend Yonsei. His talk was very inspirational, but there was not enough enthusiasm and support to make that circle a success.

I felt there was a need for a student circle to accommodate students from all academic disciplines, but I had no influential friends in other departments. Most students have friends all over the university who have come from the same high school; they mingle socially; they see each other in halls and meeting rooms. I had a unique background. Having no former high school classmates around, I found my social life limited and could not get to know other students from afar. Nevertheless, I set another goal: I would seek to make friends who were majoring in different fields of study.

Yonsei University requires all students to attend chapel once a week. In addition, six religion credits—Introduction to Christianity and Introduction to the Bible—were required for all students. I decided to make friends at chapel.

For the entire first semester after I set my friend-making goal, I made not a single friend outside the education department. A female student majoring in music sat on my right at chapel, but I knew little about music, and I could not find a mutual interest. The set on my left was assigned to a male student who seldom showed up. In September of 1968, chapel seating was rearranged for the second semester. This time a student majoring in business administration sat on my left; he became my first friend outside the education department. He introduced himself as Chang Kil Park and expressed interest in my major. He knew I was blind, but that did not matter to him. At Yonsei University in the sixties, the group of students considered the most intelligent were those enrolled in the College of Business and Economics. Their average entrance examination score is usually higher than those of the other colleges. Chang Kil placed second when he took his entrance exam.

As our friendship developed, I shared my goal of organizing an ideal student circle. He was angry to hear of the discrimination of some of the old-line clubs, and he adopted my goal. Furthermore, Chang Kil sold the idea to one of his classmates and to his roommate, a chemistry major. The four of us held a historic meeting at my house in October 1968. At that meeting we wrote a constitution and by-laws and named the circle "Yonsei Jayu Kyoyanghoe," meaning "a group of Yonsei University students dedicated to becoming free and cultivated leaders." The circle's goal was to further freedom and culture among its members through the reading and discussion of great books. We also discussed three ways to make our club a success:

(1) We were only four, but we were all top students in our major fields, and we were well known throughout the campus. We decided to write articles for "Yonsei Choonchoo," the university newspaper. The articles were widely read and attracted many student applicants.

(2) We decided our adviser must be a very famous professor. I convinced Dr. Tae Rim Yoon, Dean of the Graduate School of Education, to be our first adviser. A nationally-recognized scholar, he had presided over other universities and had been Korea's Vice-minister of Education.

(3) I secured a campus office for the club through the Dean of General Affairs, who had been instrumental in gaining permission for me to take the entrance examination. Sometimes God works in strange ways; if my application had not at first been denied, I would never have known the dean.

For the remaining three years of my campus life, I devoted much of my time and energy to the development of the club. I used my house as a second office. The rewards were great. Through circle activity, I made many friends with diverse academic and personal backgrounds, and my environment was enlarged. In its first nineteen years, Yonsei Jayu Kyoyanghoe was acknowledged as one of the best student circles at the university, with a reputation for producing academic and social leaders. Of the founding members, Dr. Kyu Hak Kyung has become a professor of business administration at Yonsei and an adviser of the club, Chang Kil Park took his Ph.D. at Texas A&M University, and Chang Koo Ji has become a business executive at a major chemical company.

My circle friends did not mind taking me anyplace they went. They even took me to Yon-Ko Jeon, which is the Yonsei University-Korea University annual sports competition. Since those two schools have traditionally produced Korea's top competition, the games get national attention. The deafening cheers, music, and noise of both student bodies were intensely exciting; I took the radio with me and experienced the total atmosphere. I also went camping, hiking, and swimming with sighted friends, and I enjoyed touring South Korea's cultural centers and other cities with them.

I graduated in 1972 with the second highest academic average. I was tremendously grateful to friends, leaders, readers, professors, the administration, and the McNeills, all of whom had shared my joys and troubles. The McNeills, who supported me in every way through college, now turned their attention to my younger brother and sister.

5
Falling in Love with a Woman of Courage

THE WORD COURAGE is often applied to soldiers, athletes, and adventurers—men and women of action who can push our admiration to great heights. Another kind of courage is the quiet courage that attracts little attention to itself and often goes unnoticed.

I want to tell you about a quiet woman who made a series of courageous decisions that do not fit into Korean social and cultural norms: volunteering to be my reader and my sighted guide, studying blind rehabilitation, changing her career to become an orientation and mobility teacher for the blind—and marrying me.

Kyoung Sook Suk was born in Seoul on May 29, 1942. Her father was a high school teacher, one of the few Koreans who was allowed to earn a B.A. degree from a Japanese college. Her mother was one of few Korean women of her time who received a high school education. Kyoung, an only child, had a happy and peaceful childhood in relative affluence.

When Kyoung was a third grader in a public school in Seoul, Communists from North Korea invaded the south, and full-scale war swept over her home. Her family moved to Kunsan, a southern harbor city. Her father was employed as a teacher, and the family remained there even after the war. She received her middle school education at Kunsan Girls' Middle School, and she is a proud alumna of Seoul National University Teachers College

Laboratory High School, the best high school in Korea at that time. Only a tiny fraction of the academically able students in the nation could pass its entrance examination.

The high school was located right across from the National Medical Center where I was hospitalized for so long. I envied the students in their uniforms. When I felt particularly moody and alone, I would go to the top of the hospital building, then one of the tallest buildings in Seoul. I had enough vision at that time to see the students, from my seventh floor vantage, coming out of the school in active, busy, happy groups. Frequently I wept, musing, "Without my eye problem I could take those entrance examinations." I never dreamed that my future wife was among the students I envied so much.

After graduating from high school, Kyoung entered Sook-myung Women's University, a school with a fine reputation for producing wise mothers and good wives as well as women leaders. Kyoung chose that university because of its tradition and image. During her early college days, she was active in service organizations. She was vice-president of the Red Cross Student Association and completed the Girl Scout leadership training program.

We met during her freshman year when I attended one of the scout meetings. Legally blind, I still had some residual vision. I could find my way to the meeting place without a cane. When Kyoung volunteered to guide me to the bus stop after the meeting, it was a courageous offer for a couple of reasons. She had never met a blind person before, and she had lived all her life in a society that avoided, shunned, and spit on its blind. Her compassion was so strong that she did not care what others might think. Basic also in Korean tradition is separation of the sexes, beginning at a very tender age. Confucius said, "Seven-year-old boys and girls should not sit together," a moral principle that has had deep root in Korean daily living. Thus, it was a very courageous thing for a girl in her late teens to offer a teenage boy a helping hand.

She did not know the correct guide techniques, nor did I. She held my left forearm, and we walked together. I can still remember seeing her face with my remaining vision, since she was so close to me. Her vivid and lively voice impressed me very much.

Kyoung's compassion was not a fleeting thing. She visited me almost every weekend, becoming my reader and guide. Eric Hoffer has some lovely words to say about compassion, "Almost all noble attributes—love, courage, faith, loyalty—can be transmuted into ruthlessness. But compassion alone can stand apart from continued traffic between good and evil. It is antitoxin of the soul" (*Saturday Review*, 24 Nov. 1979).

When Kyoung was in high school, her father died of a stroke. Her mother began suffering from tuberculosis when Kyoung was in her sophomore year in college. Family hardships finally forced Kyoung to discontinue her studies and take a clerical job at Kangwon Provincial Government in Chuncheon. While she was in Chuncheon, we exchanged letters every week and often visited.

One summer day I took a train to visit Kyoung. She took me to the nearby River Soyang. In my childhood we had lived near the Han, and I enjoyed swimming in the river in summer, skating on it in winter. While sitting there on the bank of the Soyang with Kyoung, I had a strong desire to swim again. I had not been in the water since becoming blind and would have liked company, but Kyoung did not swim. This meant I would have to go alone, but I decided to try it.

It felt good to be in the water again. I could swim very well, but I was not sure of my direction, and soon I was swimming away from Kyoung. She yelled at me, but I did not hear her. She was frantic. Finally I realized I had almost crossed the river—several hundred yards wide at that point. I could hear people very close on the other bank. Suddenly, to my embarrassment, a nearby fisherman yelled, "Are you drunk? Get on the boat right now!" From that experience I learned how important is the concept of time and distance for a blind person. With an accurate concept of time and distance, I would have avoided embarrassment for me and a terrible fright for Kyoung.

While working in Chuncheon, Kyoung kept trying to find a job in Seoul. Finally she got a new clerical position at Samho Trading Company, one of the largest of Korea's international trading concerns.

In Korea it is customary for parents or friends to arrange interviews between prospective bride and bridegroom. Since Kyoung did not have a steady boyfriend, her mother and friends tried to arrange such interviews for her during her employment at the trading company. She had promised me she would only marry a person of whom I approved, and I had very high expectations for her. Frequently I opposed those whom she looked upon with favor, which made it very difficult for her to find a marriage partner.

About a year after she started her job in Seoul, on one of her visits to me, she said she wanted to develop a new career as a blind rehabilitation specialist. She was well paid and was satisfied with her job, but she had decided to devote her entire life to promoting blind rehabilitation. I felt her philosophy and personality were ideal for such a career and encouraged the idea. Ever since my discharge from the hospital, Dr. Koo had continued his interest in my progress. He became chief ophthalmologist at Catholic Medical Center and did research at the Armed Forces Institute of Pathology in Washington, D.C. I thought Dr. Koo might be of help to Kyoung and took her to his office to share her courageous decision.

"I have seen you guide Mr. Kang for a long time," said Dr. Koo. "I consider your ability to do so one of your many assets. I am sure you can make it, Miss Suk. My judgment is based on my observation that you do not mind others' negative reactions when you help him. You are truly dedicated and committed. Blind rehabilitation needs individuals like you."

We were very pleased. We knew that Dr. Koo was in a position to help implement Kyoung's ambitious plan. The doctor had, in fact, recently met some American leaders in the field of blind rehabilitation. He told us about Dr. Norman Yoder, Commissioner of the Pennsylvania State Office for the Blind. Dr. Yoder, Dr. Koo said, was adventitiously blind and had a Ph.D. from Ohio State University; he was a recognized authority throughout the United States in rehabilitation for the blind. Dr. Koo suggested we write him.

We went directly to Kyoung's home to write Dr. Yoder. Kyoung's letter said, in part:

> . . . When I learned that Young Woo was blind, I wanted to become his eyes. I believed that he could see through my eyes. I wanted to comfort and guide him as long as I am alive. For the last six years I have tried to do this for him.
>
> I am under great pressure to get married. This implies that the time will come when I have to leave him. I have recently realized that he will become twice blind when I leave him. He must not depend on me. He must stand independently. Prejudice and discrimination against the blind is rather severe. Even though my "brother" is very bright he has very little chance for his occupational success (to gain a Ph.D.) because of his blindness.
>
> In order to help Young Woo achieve his life goal and devote the rest of my life to promoting education of the Korean blind, I would like to study in the United States. I shall greatly appreciate your guidance and help.

Apparently Dr. Yoder brought Kyoung's letter to the attention of his advisory board. Among other members, Mrs. Catharine Craig and Dr. Atton G. Kloss were interested in helping her come to the United States for training. Mrs. Craig, wife of leading ophthalmologist Dr. Paul C. Craig, holds an honorary doctorate in the humanities from Albright College in Pennsylvania. She was a friend of the late Dr. Hellen Kim, a leader in modern Korean education and former president of Ehwa Women's University. She was president of the Women's Auxiliary of the American Medical Society and has known outstanding Korean ophthalmologists such as Dr. Koo through her husband. Dr. Kloss was a

Falling in Love 43

college president before becoming superintendent of Western Pennsylvania School for Blind Children. He became interested in education for the blind because he had blind twin sons.

Dr. Yoder, Mrs. Craig, and Dr. Kloss worked out a special plan to bring Kyoung to the United States for one year—October 1967 through September 1968. Dr. Kloss assumed legal responsibility as official sponsor; Mrs. Craig assumed financial responsibility. Kyoung was housed in the homes of members of the Pennsylvania Medical Society as she traveled to different schools and agencies for the blind. It was a marvelous opportunity.

Dr. Yoder designed her educational program which included:

(1) General review of government-sponsored rehabilitation programs.

(2) Study of the rehabilitation of the adult blind, field visits with professional staff, and observation of the development of employment for the blind.

(3) Visits to rehabilitation centers offering mobility, daily living activities, communication skills, and other services leading to independence.

(4) Exposure to the Western Pennsylvania School for Blind Children, working with severely disabled blind children, a visit to Overbrook School for the Blind, and emphasis on academics.

(5) Work with the Royer-Graves School for the Blind (mentally retarded).

(6) A series of exposures to private agencies serving the blind in social service, mobility, blindness prevention, and sheltered workshops.

On September 30, 1967 in California, while enroute to Pennsylvania, Kyoung met Mr. and Mrs. McNeill.

In Pittsburgh, a story in the *Post-Gazette* told about "A Korean Woman Here to Help Her Blind: A Duty for Homeland." She found Korean friends in Pittsburgh, among them high school and university classmates.

Kyoung made an indelible impression on the people she worked with in the United States. Mrs. Craig said, "She does not know the meaning of the word *impossible*. When the going gets hard, she goes into low gear and keeps on." Dr. and Mrs. Craig informally adopted her. They urged her to go after a college degree, and upon her return to Korea they financed her college years until she was awarded a B.A. degree in elementary education at Sookmyung Women's University in 1972.

On her way home, she stopped for a month in Japan to study educational and rehabilitation programs in Tokyo and Osaka. Dr. Koo arranged that, and when she got back to Seoul, Kyoung helped the doctor establish the Sight Library for the Blind at his hospital. She developed new programs at the Rehabilitation Center for the Blind of Korea, where I had learned to type and read Braille.

Kyoung was still under social pressure. In Korea she was considered at an age when it was essential that she marry. We still had not resolved our relationship. Then, on December 22, 1968, Kyoung and I were walking toward the home of my aunt, my mother's elder sister, the only relative with whom I have had close ties since being blinded. Kyoung had been back in Korea three weeks.

"I have been waiting," I said to her, "for you to marry someone you really love." In Korea younger siblings usually must wait until the elder siblings marry, and so I was speaking as a younger brother when I said, "I'm looking forward to my turn."

Kyoung seemed startled. After a minute she asked, "Have you met a girlfriend at Yonsei University?"

She had been out of the country fourteen months, and many changes had occurred for both of us. I had become an honor student at one of the nation's most prestigious universities. She had met many blind Americans who were successful in various fields. She had learned that blindness was no handicap to marriage, given other satisfactory conditions.

From the question and tone of her voice, I realized with sudden clarity that she did not want me to have a girlfriend! She did not want to leave me. My heart leaped.

"Yes I have," I lied. "I have more than one." I listened very carefully for her reaction. There was only silence. Kyoung seemed confused and startled.

"If you do not want me to have other girlfriends," I said, "why not marry me?" That was my way out of the situation: if she found my proposal embarrassing, she could treat it as a joke. Her continued silence made me realize she was taking it seriously.

"Would it be possible?" she asked softly.

I knew why she asked the question. We had considered ourselves brother and sister for six years. "Of course it is possible," I said. "We are not blood related." For the first time, I threw my arms around her.

And Kyoung said, "Yes!"

Our pseudo-sibling relationship ended, and our romance began, although we had been in love in one respect for so long.

On that day, I promised to make Kyoung a very happy wife. I named her Suk Woon Ok, which means "stone silver pearl," a name that reflects my life philosophy. Kyoung's family name was Suk, which means "stone." I regarded the first ten years after we met as the period of Suk (Stone). In that period we had to overcome difficulties, deprivations, and suffering. The second ten years I designated the period of Woon (Silver), a time for preparing ourselves for achieving a common life goal. The third ten years are Ok (Pearl), when we devote much of our time and energy to promoting the ideals of human dignity and service for the betterment of society. Since that fateful December day, Kyoung has preferred her new name. She is better known by that name among Korean friends and by the Korean public, and, of course, that was the name we used at our wedding ceremony.

The period of Stone lasted another three years after the marriage proposal. Many difficulties and obstacles still lay ahead for us. We had made our decision, but we could not implement it until my graduation from Yonsei University. In those three years, something could happen to jeopardize our new relationship.

The influence of parents, relatives, and friends on marriage in Korea is tremendous. We informed a very limited circle of friends of our decision, including Dr. and Mrs. Craig, Dr. Koo, Rev. Kim, and Mr. and Mrs. McNeill. We did not even tell Kyoung's mother. Generally, our friends' reactions were favorable and encouraging.

Our love grew and matured against incredible odds, its foundation cemented in an extremely difficult situation. To avoid negative reactions, our engagement was announced just two weeks before the wedding. It was a shock to many people and disappointed many of Kyoung's relatives. Some of her friends considered her crazy and some even quit associating with her. Kyoung's mother was disappointed at first but gradually became convinced we could make a good marriage.

In the fourth week of February 1972, we were principals in three of life's major ceremonies. On February 21 I earned my B.A. degree in education from Yonsei University. On February 25 Kyoung received her B.A. degree in elementary education from Sookmyung Women's University. On February 26 we were married in the auditorium of the Christian Building in Seoul. The events were reported widely in Korean news media and were hailed as inspirational by many.

Some of my university friends planned and supervised the wedding. Three hundred people attended. The Yemel Choir (composed of nonmusic graduates of Ehwa Girls' High School) sang a festive song. The ceremony was taped, and we listen to it each anniversary; it reminds us of the devotion of friends, their help and support.

The first ten years of our acquaintance—the period of Stone—ended three months after our wedding. We went to Pusan, Korea's second largest city, for our honeymoon. It is famous for beautiful beaches, but we were there in the middle of winter, and the beach was very quiet. Fortunately the weather was mild, and we sat on the sand, listening to the waves and dreaming impossible dreams for the next ten years—the period of Silver.

6

The First Blind Korean Ph.D.

AS I STOOD WAITING TO RECEIVE my doctoral degree from the University of Pittsburgh on April 25, 1976, I was just one of hundreds of doctoral candidates, yet I felt my very presence at the ceremony shouted a triumphant message: "Through the goodness of God and the help of ever so many friends, I am here! I am part of a world I once believed was lost to me forever!" At my side was my exultant wife, Kyoung. University officials had given her special permission to take part in the procession as my guide.

The day of April 25th was the culmination of a goal set during my junior year at Yonsei University. Setting the goal was easy. The hard part was finding money for study abroad. I wrote letters to all my American friends—and I had a considerable number, largely through Kyoung. No luck. My junior year passed without finding a sponsor. As a last resort, I wrote to Mrs. Gwen Zarfoss.

Mrs. Zarfoss, one of Kyoung's friends, and I had met briefly in Seoul in 1968 at the airport when I went to see her and her husband off at the end of their Korean visit. I was impressed at that time by the number and the importance of her Korean friends, among them a navy admiral and several other high-ranking officers. Both Mr. and Mrs. Zarfoss were busy talking with their friends, but she very graciously managed some time for me. Her Korean friends wondered how she could be so nice to a blind student.

I was greatly encouraged when I received an immediate reply from her. In her letter, she introduced me to Mr. William T. Powell, manager of a district office for Pennsylvania's Commission for the Visually Handicapped, who was also governor-elect of Rotary District 728 in northwestern Pennsylvania. He helped me get a Rotary International scholarship.

In May 1972, I received official notice of admission from the International Student Office of the University of Pittsburgh and notice of the financial commitment from Rotary International District 728. I applied for a student passport—only to suffer another shock.

In order to get a student passport, Koreans had to take examinations required by the Ministry of Education; I was told I could not take them because I was blind. The ministry had a regulation which specifically barred physically or mentally handicapped individuals. No official explanation was ever offered, but it is my guess that the government did not want any Korean traveling abroad who might be considered a "discredit to the nation." At that time, Korean officialdom did not realize that cultivated peoples respect the ideals of equal rights and human dignity, that in developed nations the handicapped are as much producers as are others.

I took my problem to Dr. U Sang Lee at the American Korean Foundation in Seoul. As a part-time faculty member at Yonsei University, he had been one of my teachers and knew my academic record. He suggested Yonsei University and the American Korean Foundation jointly request the Minister of Education to rescind the regulation. He wrote the letter and got the signature of the foundation president. The university president, Dr. Dae Sun Park, signed the letter without question.

Minister Kwan Shik Min approved the request as soon as Dr. Lee submitted it, and in this way I became the first disabled student to be permitted to leave Korea to study. Now the door was opened to other disabled people.

When I applied for a visa for Kyoung and me, the American consul did not even interview us. The notice of university admission, the notarized letter of invitation from Mr. Powell, and our passports were sufficient.

In August 1972, we flew from Kimpo International Airport to Los Angeles. For the first time, I met my foster parents, Frazier and Elsie McNeill, who financed nine years of my education in Korea, including four years at Yonsei. I talked to their church congregation, Mr. McNeill's Rotary Club, and the Los Angeles Goodwill Industries about my experiences. Despite my apprehension at finally meeting them face to face, we had a wonderful visit.

At 7 A.M. on September 5, we arrived at Pittsburgh International Airport and were met by Rev. Philip Park. "*Annyung Hashibnika,*" he said, with a slight accent. In Korean that means "How are you?"

"Were you a missionary in Korea?" I asked.

"No," he said. "My grandparents came from Korea."

My adviser at Pittsburgh was to be Dr. Ralph Peabody, with whom Rev. Park's wife had studied. When Rev. Park heard from Dr. Peabody that I was coming, he volunteered to meet us. He helped me register the day we arrived, and we stayed for two weeks in the Parks' nice big home until we found an apartment. Kyoung, of course, had been in Pittsburgh before. Her friends from the Pennsylvania Medical Women's Auxiliary also helped us in many ways.

I always knew that Pittsburgh was one of the major steel manufacturing centers of the world. Soon after arriving, I learned that Pittsburgh also is a cultural, educational, and economic center, ranking third—following New York and Chicago—in the number of major industry headquarters. I was also impressed to learn that the University of Pittsburgh was among fifty leading universities, according to the American Association of Universities' ranking, and had a Learning Research and Development

Center that was one of the largest and best of its kind in the United States.

I went to my first class in Pittsburgh on September 6. The professor was Dr. Peabody. At Yonsei University, my minor field of study was English. I had never received a grade lower than A in English and had even obtained a certificate to teach English in Korea, and of course I has passed the TOEFL (Test of English as a Foreign Language) to be admitted to the University of Pittsburgh. I was very proud of my knowledge of English, but in the first class I could understand only half of the lecture.

On the second day, I was the only student waiting in the classroom. For ten minutes no one came. I began to wonder. Then I heard someone.

"Where are the other students?" he asked.

"I don't know."

"I'll check it out," he said. He came back in a few minutes and told me the classroom had been changed. "I was absent last week," he said, "were you?"

I was so embarrassed that I said yes. Apparently Dr. Peabody had made the announcement in class, and it was part of the lecture I failed to understand.

At registration, Dr. Peabody told me the Advanced Educational Psychology course could be waived if I passed the test. I received all A's in educational psychology at Yonsei, and so I chose to take the test, which had many multiple choice questions. Unfortunately, I could not understand some of them as they were read to me by an American woman, and I failed the test—the first test I had ever failed. My pride would not permit me to take the course. Instead, I waited until the following term when my understanding of American English was better, took the test again, and passed. The course was waived.

One day in my first week, I visited Dr. Mary Moore at her office. During our conversation, there were phrases and sentences I could not understand. She repeated them, very slowly and very clearly, but I still did not get it.

"By Christmas," she said, "you will understand me very well."

Despite her encouragement, I was frustrated and embarrassed, but seven weeks later I scored second highest in her midterm test in a course called Anatomy and Physiology of the Eye, a difficult course even for Americans. My test grade was good for two reasons. Even though I was having troubles with spoken English, I had an excellent foundation in the written word, so I could read and write English with no difficulty. Then, too, I was early surrounded by a cadre of competent and compassionate friends who wanted to help.

One day a student named Vince asked what he could do. I asked him to show me how to do the new class assignment each week, and he did that throughout the term. Another friend was Dianne Wormsley, who had been a teacher at a school for the blind in New York for three years before entering Pitt's graduate program. For the full year until I completed my master's degree work, Dianne gave me a carbon copy of the notes she typed every night. A volunteer transcriber translated her notes into Braille.

Textbooks were available either in tape or Braille. Some taped texts were borrowed from the Recording for the Blind in New York, and Dr. Moore arranged for others to be taped by volunteers from among fellow parishioners at Pleasant Hill United Presbyterian Church. Some technical textbooks were translated into Baille by volunteers of the Rodef Shalom Temple Sisterhood. Many live readers helped me at libraries or at our apartment. Mrs. Esther Morrow bought me a cassette recorder, which I am still using, as a Christmas present that first year in the United States.

All the volunteers who helped me are either professionals or married to professionals. They are truly service oriented. Fifteen years after they first read for me, taped books, or translated them into Braille, we still have close contact, and so my blindness served as a catalyst for many friendships.

At Yonsei I had many friends willing to help me move from class to class. As a matter of fact, they picked me up at home in the morning and dropped me off at the end of the day. I had no formal mobility training—it did not exist then in Seoul. Kyoung, actually, is the one who established the first such program in the nation, at the Rehabilitation Center for the Blind of Korea in 1972. In the United States, most blind college students get the proper training before going to school; mobility training is an integral part of their experience. Because they were used to independent blind people, most American students did not at first offer to guide or help. Some of my classmates kidded me, in fact, about Kyoung, who stayed close as my shadow. She even came to my classes. "You don't want her to leave," they said, "because you haven't been married very long."

True, I enjoyed having Kyoung nearby. She was an immense help. But the situation was changing. I had to become independently mobile—and soon. Kyoung was expecting our first child, due in April. The urgency led me to approach Dr. Bruce Blasch, who was teaching a course called Orientation and Mobility for Teachers. Dr. Blasch arranged for one of his mobility students, Ad Lee, to earn his internship credits by training me. Ad was a competent and hard-working instructor. During my second term, from January to April of 1973, he taught me orientation concepts, other sensory development and use, and long cane techniques. The cane techniques are also called Hoover techniques because they were originally developed by Dr. Richard Hoover, an ophthalmologist at Johns Hopkins University. By the time our baby arrived, I was entirely mobile on and around the campus.

The two-hour intensive mobility training three or four times a week made me very tired. After those sessions, I still had to study, but my blindness made it possible for me to rest and study at the same time. Lying on the bed or couch, I would put my Braille book on my stomach and study. Since I could study without lights, no matter the hour, I did not disturb Kyoung in the sensitive latter days of her pregnancy. Clearly it was a case where blindness was not a handicap, but an advantage.

Despite language and mobility problems, I earned three A's and one B during the first term; four A's in the second.

Toward the end of March 1973, Dr. and Mrs. William Ridgeway sent us prepaid airplane tickets and an invitation to their home in Lancaster County, Pennsylvania. The doctor had been a family physician, and Mrs. Ridgeway, an officer of the Pennsylvania Medical Women's Auxiliary, had been a friend of Kyoung's since she trained in the United States.

We toured the countryside surrounding the Ridgeways' home, and we were most impressed by the Amish and their way of life. We never dreamed that people in a country as developed as the United States actually lived without material conveniences. We visited a farm market that reminded me of my childhood. Once every five days, there used to be a farm market in my hometown. Mrs. Ridgeway took us to a farm where the patriarch was a Ridgeway patient. He showed us every hospitality, and he read us a poem that moved us deeply.

Mrs. Catharine Craig visited us at the Ridgeway home. It was my first meeting with her, even though we had exchanged letters since 1967. I expressed to Mrs. Craig my desire for and interest in entering a Ph.D. program. She said, "You will be able to make a greater contribution at the international level with a doctoral degree," and she promised to do everything she could to help.

Recognizing that Kyoung would deliver within a month, Dr. Ridgeway asked what we would name the baby. I said we had not decided, that we planned to discuss one boy's name and one girl's name on the return flight to Pittsburgh. Jokingly he said, "Don't think of a girl's name. I am sure you will have a baby boy." He was right, but we discussed two names on the plane anyway. I suggested Paul and Martha. Kyoung agreed.

Since I had resolved my psychological and spiritual conflict by identifying my blindness with Paul's thorn, I wanted to name my son after the Apostle. Paul also has a Korean name. We called him Jin Suk, which means "Foundation Stone of Truth." Since I believe that the Apostle Paul has been a foundation stone of truth, I decided to give our Paul a comparable Korean name. Jin Suk, of course, encompasses still another meaning for us, since Kyoung's maiden name was Suk.

Our baby was due in mid-April. Kyoung was to deliver at Magee Women's Hospital, and we had already requested a volunteer from the Pittsburgh Blind Association to give me rides so that I could visit mother and baby. On the evening of April 22, Kyoung began to have labor pains. One of the Korean students in our apartment building drove us to the hospital, but the doctor told me it would be at least ten hours before the baby arrived. At his suggestion, I returned to the apartment with my friend. For hours I could not go to sleep. Finally, in the wee hours of the morning, I dozed.

The shrill ring of the telephone woke me at 6:30 A.M. A nurse said, "Your wife delivered a healthy baby boy at 5:45 A.M. He weighs seven pounds, seven ounces. Congratulations!" She said that mother and baby were fine, that I need not hurry to the hospital. I decided to phone the news to close friends.

My first call was to Mrs. Crozier, a trustee of the University of Pittsburgh and a close friend of Mrs. Craig. She had stimulated the interest of several members of the Pennsylvania Medical Society in us and had helped in many ways, "I will make phone calls to other friends for you," she said. "You go to see Kyoung and that new baby."

I telephoned the volunteer who was to give me rides to the hospital; she picked me up in less than ten minutes. My chauffeur was the wife of Dr. McCaslin who chaired the department of Ophthalmology at the Eye/Ear Hospital in Pittsburgh, a friend of both Mrs. Craig and Mrs. Crozier. Mrs. McCaslin drove me back and forth twice a day until Kyoung and Paul came home to the apartment five days later.

At 4 P.M. on the day Paul was born, Mrs. Crozier telephoned me and said, "The University Center for International Studies'

Asian Studies Program has just granted you a full tuition scholarship for your Ph.D. program!" On my behalf, she had contacted Dr. William Dorrill, the Asian Studies Program director, and convinced him of the need and the benefit. "This morning," said Mrs. Crozier, "you gave me good news. Now I am giving you good news!"

On May 25, 1973, I was a main speaker at the annual conference of Rotary District 728 in Titusville, PA. Mr. Powell, following that conference, wrote the Rotary Foundation of Rotary International asking for a foundation scholarship. That scholarship, granted in August, was separate from that of the Asian Studies Program and provided living expenses for a year while I worked toward a Ph.D.

September 1972 through August 1973 was an unbelievably busy, productive, and rewarding year:

—I earned a master of education degree.
—I was awarded a full tuition scholarship for the doctoral program.
—I was awarded a second scholarship that would pay our living expenses while I worked for the doctorate.
—I learned to be independently mobile on and about the Pittsburgh campus.
—We became parents.

The first year of the Ph.D. program passed without significant difficulty, but the second year brought new problems. The Asian Studies scholarship would continue to pay my tuition, but the Rotary Foundation money for living expenses was exhausted. I had to find a way to support my family.

I began looking for a part-time job as a masseur. Once I had hated the idea of becoming a masseur. Now attaining the Ph.D. was worth any sacrifice, and I had no other skills. I telephoned all the health clubs in Pittsburgh. The Hebrew Young Men's Association was the only one that expressed interest. But when I was interviewed, the interviewer said, "Your hands are too small and weak to give an effective massage to huge Americans."

Mrs. McCaslin suggested Kyoung try for a cleaning job at her husband's hospital. She said the pay was high enough that we would be able to afford a babysitter for Paul, who was one year old. Kyoung was willing to leave him with someone else if she could help solve our problem, but the hospital personnel department told us Kyoung's student's wife's visa would not allow her to work. At the Pittsburgh office of the Immigration and Naturalization Service, the officer in charge refused—with calculated rudeness—to grant a temporary work permit. "There is," he said, "no exception to the law."

The day after our disappointment at the immigration office, we were invited to dinner at the home of an American family who, although they already had three sons, had adopted three Korean orphans. Richard Fox was a buyer for Gimbel department stores. His wife, Evelyn, was a very busy mother and housewife. Two of their Korean children were brother and sister. They suspected the sister was deaf, and they enlisted our help to ascertain that she had a physical problem, that she was not withdrawing because of the language difference. Unfortunately, the little girl was indeed deaf.

Because of our frequent contacts and their continuing interest in Korean culture, we became great friends with the Foxes. In October 1974, we went with them to a picnic for adoptive parents at a park near the campus. When we arrived, Kyoung said, "There is an unusual couple here. The husband is sighted and the wife is blind. He is pushing her swing." Kyoung guided me to them, and we became fast friends.

Ceinwen King-Smith, a Christian minister's daughter, was born blind. She and Sandford King-Smith met when they were students at Stanford University. He asked her to help him with Russian; she taped her notes from Braille; they fell in love. After they were married, they both attended Harvard—he to study international tax law, she to work on her master's degree in education. Sandy was an international tax lawyer at United States Steel Corporation when we met; Ceinwen, a math teacher at the Hebrew Academy. She related proudly how, despite her blindness, she got teaching jobs in Brazil and Poland when her husband was assigned to those countries. They had two children, Heather, 5, and Martin, 4.

In a matter of months, the King-Smiths invited us to move into the second floor of their house and to share meals with them. Kyoung was to do the dishes and take care of Heather and Martin, as well as Paul, whenever they were away. A cleaning lady came in once a week. The King-Smith's home was truly an international house. Besides us, there were two other foreign students, one from Egypt, the other from Brazil. We stayed with them for a year. About the same age, we had a lot of common interests. On weekends they sometimes took us swimming. Paul had fun with his older playmates.

Rev. Park, who met us at the airport when we first got to Pittsburgh, had a new job at the New York headquarters of the United Presbyterian Church of the United States of America. He influenced the Pittsburgh Presbyterial Society to adopt my family's living expenses as a church project. The society set up a tax deductible fund in Pittsburgh Presbytery and sought contributions.

Mrs. Jane Rosenberger, a society board member and an elder of Woodland United Presbyterian Church, was a prime mover for the fund. She and her family, friends, church, and many other churches contributed. So did our personal friends, even those who were not Presbyterians.

In February 1975, Mrs. Dorothy Fulton, secretary of the Presbyterial Society, invited me to be a main speaker at the national board meeting of Presbyterian Women. I talked about the needs of the disabled in Korea and of what I would like to do about them. The talk made me many friends and heightened interest in the fund. The fund drive was so successful that our living expenses were covered for the remaining fourteen months of study.

The oral defense of my dissertation was February 26, 1976. Coincidentally, it was our fourth wedding anniversary. I felt more nervous than when I took the comprehensive exam the year before. Five members of the dissertation committee finally finished asking questions, and Dr. Peabody, the chairman, asked me to wait outside the room as they voted. In a few minutes, he came out. "Dr. Kang, I am the first to congratulate you on becoming a doctor!"

On my way back to our apartment, my thoughts were of my mother. She had died eight hours after receiving the terrifying news that her son would be blind for life. If she could only have known that her blind son would, in fifteen years, become the first blind Korean Ph.D. I could not stop weeping. Over and over I expressed my thanks to her for her endless prayers, prayers that had been answered.

7

God Opens a Better Door

I KNEW MY GOAL to teach at a university at home in Korea flew in the teeth of centuries of tradition, thoughtless discrimination, ignorance, injustice, and innate cruelty toward the disabled. It is reported that there are 450 million disabled persons in the world. In the United States alone, one of every seven persons is disabled—35 million Americans. Only one out of every ten school children is handicapped, but by age fifty-four, one of every four persons is disabled to some degree. In the United States, section 504 of the Rehabilitation Act of 1973 prohibits discrimination against the disabled solely based on disability. Thus far such legal protection is the impossible dream of the disabled in Korea.

In December 1975, four months before my graduation, I began to look for a teaching position in Korea. I wrote letters to Yonsei professors who had taught me and to personal friends who had helped me develop self-worth and a fighting spirit. Dr. William Dorrill, who had granted me full tuition during my Ph.D. study, knew several university presidents in Seoul. I wrote to each, my letter buttressed by Dr. Dorrill's endorsement.

Dr. Paul Masoner headed a team of American professors evaluating the Korea Education Development Institute in 1975. With him was Dr. John Bolvin, Associate Dean of the School of Education at Pittsburgh, who had taught me a course called

Education Research. Both of them believed Korea needs competent, trained persons to establish special education and rehabilitation programs, and they promised they would do everything in their power to secure a faculty position for me. They were confident they could accomplish that mission, and their confidence infected me.

After graduation, I had no income. Dr. and Mrs. Craig were so concerned for my family that they personally supported us for four months, May through August 1976.

My letters to Korea produced no job.

Richard and Evelyn Fox, the couple with three adopted Korean children, who had become our very good friends, offered to share their home with us. We stayed with them for two months in those troubled times.

While Dr. Masoner's team was still in the Orient, our second son, Christopher, was born. We had planned for him, because we were sure I would have a good job by the time he was born; we would be out of financial crisis. Our hopes did not materialize, and Chris arrived June 15, 1976, in a time of confusion and desperation. This time I was with Kyoung in the delivery room at Magee Women's Hospital. At 5:45 P.M., the doctor handed me the baby. "A healthy boy," he said. As soon as Kyoung saw me holding him, she cried out with glee, "He looks the same as Paul!" She sounded like she had totally forgotten her labor pains.

Dr. Masoner returned to the States empty-handed. He could find no job for me in Korea. Our last hope turned to despair, anger, and frustration. I had to admit failure. I felt betrayed by the country of my birth, the country I trusted and loved. Worse, in August 1976, my United States' student visa expired. It could not be extended because I was no longer a student. Dr. Masoner suggested I go back to the university to broaden my employment opportunities by taking a postdoctoral program in Foundations of Education. At his recommendation, I was granted a one-semester fellowship from the School of Education. I took nine credits: History of American Higher Learning, Philosophy of Education, and Sociology of Education. Since I was a student again, my student visa was extended for a year.

I still had no way of supporting my family, and the hope of teaching Foundations of Education in Korea was dim, at best. I had never intended to seek a job in the United States—I felt that would be a betrayal of my country and of other handicapped persons in Korea. I was fully aware that many friends had helped me attain a doctoral degree because I told them I wanted to establish special education and rehabilitation programs in Korea.

Back in school, I started applying for positions in the States. Dr. Masoner and other faculty members endorsed my efforts, but no employer was willing to hire a foreigner with a student visa. They did not want to go through the lengthy, complicated legal process required; to hire foreigners, they had to prove no qualified United States workers were available for the position. I was interviewed several times from September through November 1976, but there were no job offers.

Richard Fox suggested Kyoung open a store to support our family until I could find a job. He and Evelyn bought a small building, housing three apartments and a small grocery, in our name. They told us we could repay them when we were able. They gave us the store, in fact, without legal recourse. If we were not able to pay them back, they had no signed documents, no legal trail that would force us to do so. The risk they took was a material measure of their friendship.

On December 1, 1976, we moved into one of the three apartments and began preparations to go into the grocery business. Most foreign students have at least a secondhand automobile when they study in the States, but we had never been able to afford a car. Kyoung would need one to be a grocery proprietor, so we purchased a six-year-old Plymouth Reliant. Mary Lou Ende, my volunteer reader, taught Kyoung to drive. Paul, at three-and-a-half, was very excited at the prospect of helping his mom sell groceries.

One week after moving to the apartment, I received a phone

call from the city schools of Gary, Indiana, for a job interview. Fortunately, the interviewer did not ask what kind of visa I had. I was offered a contract to start work on January 3, the same day Kyoung was supposed to open the store.

I got back to Pittsburgh by bus at 1 A.M. It was raining hard. I took a taxi home, partly because I did not want to wake Kyoung and the children, partly because I wanted to deliver in person the good news that she did not have to become a storekeeper.

Kyoung was up, waiting for the phone to ring. "Did they ask you what kind of visa you have?" she asked. I did not answer. I just told her to get ready to move. She refused to believe it until I showed her the signed contract.

Dr. Peabody, my academic adviser, wrote a letter certifying that I needed practical training to complete my educational work. With that certification, I obtained a temporary work permit from Immigration and Naturalization.

We moved to Gary on January 2, 1977. It was snowing hard New Year's Day, the day we had planned to move, and it was still snowing on the 2nd. Kyoung had never driven on a highway before, except under driving instructor supervision. Now she had to drive 450 miles in a snowstorm. We did not have a choice. So we prayed fervently to God and started out for an unknown world. Paul sat in front with his mother, I sat in the back seat holding Chris. Fortunately, there were not many cars on the highway because the weather was so bad and it was the New Year. Kyoung gained confidence with each passing mile. It usually takes eight or nine hours to make the Pittsburgh-Gary trip, but this time it took us twelve hours. When we got to Gary it was dark. We stayed one night in a motel, then I started work while Kyoung went apartment hunting.

Six months later we returned to Pittsburgh to sell the grocery/apartment building. We were very pleased to return the money to the Fox family, complete with bank-rate interest.

A few months before we moved to Indiana, Dean Hak Soo

Kim of Kyongbuk National University's College of Education visited the University of Pittsburgh. I gave him my résumé and told him I was interested in a job at his or any other Korean university. When he returned to Korea, he discussed my qualifications with Dr. Tae Young Rhee, president of Taegu University. These two men are among the pioneers and leaders in special education in Korea. Dean Kim received the first doctoral degree in special education ever granted in Korea.

Dr. Rhee's father, Rev. Young Shik Rhee, who founded Taegu University, was actively involved in the independence movement during the Japanese occupation and was a political prisoner for many years. Once he had as a cellmate a deaf man, also a political prisoner. Through that chance meeting, Rev. Rhee came to realize that disabled persons could make valuable contributions to society if they were educated. After Korea was liberated from Japan, he established special schools for different categories of handicapped children and youth. That led to a need for trained professionals to work with the handicapped, and in 1956 he established a small college to train such professionals, a college based on the principles of light, love, and freedom. Dr. Rhee, after his education in Japan, joined his father.

In the last thirty–one years Dr. Rhee has developed that small college into one of the largest universities in Korea. Under his remarkable leadership, Taegu University has become a Korean center of special education and social welfare for the disabled. It has nine colleges, three graduate schools, eleven attached institutes plus an attached research institute, five attached schools, and other affiliations.

Korea's interim president, Kyu Hwa Choi, visited Taegu University in 1980. He was so impressed and inspired, he asked Dr. Rhee what he could do to help. "We need," said Dr. Rhee, "a Braille library to serve all the blind people, nationwide."

President Choi granted a very large fund, with which the Taegu University Braille Library was established. Among its services, the library prints and distributes Braille textbooks at elementary and secondary school levels for all thirteen schools for the blind in South Korea.

In January 1977 I received a job offer from Dr. Rhee. He had sent it to my Pittsburgh address, and it was forwarded, arriving two weeks after I started to work in Gary. If it had come a month or two earlier, I would have been settled in Taegu. Instead, I wrote, "I am very sorry that I cannot accept your kind offer at this time."

Six months later, Dr. Rhee visited me in Indiana, interviewed me, and offered a teaching job on the summer faculty. In addition, he appointed me Taegu University's United States–based Associate Dean of the College of Education. In that capacity, I have been recruiting faculty members and inviting visiting American faculty lecturers to the university to promote international exchange.

When I took my teacher-consultant position with the Gary public schools, I had authorization only for six months of "practical training," a permit that could not be extended. I applied for an immigrant visa, which for Koreans is usually limited to the immediate relatives of United States citizens or to war refugees. I was neither, but there is a "third category"—professionals meeting certain criteria. By proving that I had a job for which I was trained and qualified and that no qualified United States worker was available for the job, I gained permanent residence in August 1978, an immigrant visa that would eventually lead to United States citizenship. Kyoung was granted permanent residence as my wife. Our children were already citizens by virtue of birth in the United States. As soon as Kyoung was granted permanent residence, she got a teaching position in Gary.

A year and a half after we were settled in Indiana, I became an adjunct professor at Northeastern Illinois University in Chicago. Since then I have been teaching educators and other school professionals "Psychology of Exceptional Children," a course required of all professional school personnel in Illinois.

I have also become an international public speaker and lay evangelist. One year I lectured and preached in Canada, Japan, Korea, and the United States. If God had not closed the door to my return to Korea, my teaching would have been limited to Taegu University.

Since 1978 my academic influence in Korea has been increasing. I have taught scores of doctoral students who are now on university and college faculties. I can do more now for Korea in five weeks each year than I would have been able to do in an entire year as a full-time faculty member. Because of my international recognition I am more heard than if I were a hometown teacher.

I am very grateful to God for having given me the opportunity to promote noble human values—normalization, equal rights, and full participation in society for the handicapped—through teaching and consultation in Gary's public school system and Northeastern Illinois University. Many teachers, administrators, and others have thanked me, a blind man, for helping them; the sighted, to see things they had never seen before.

It is now the fifth year since the start of the stage of our lives called Pearl. In the period of Pearl, we are to glorify God, feel rewarded by our accomplishments, guide our children, accomplish more for humanity, and be of service to others. It was not just a coincidence that in 1982 I joined the Rotary Club, began to write this book, and started to broaden the scope of my teaching. That was the year of the beginning of our ten years of Pearl.

I expect more miracles in the remainder of my life. Once so fearful, I am sure now of God's love and purposes. God has used so many loving Christian people to reveal plans for my life and to redeem my suffering. My desire is to continue this chain of love by helping handicapped people who are in despair as I once was, by giving them a chance to hope as I now hope.

8

The World My Blindness Creates

MANY PEOPLE WONDER what blindness is like . . . what it means . . . what it does. They speculate.

I am usually surprised at their distorted perceptions. Let me describe a few essentials from my experience of living blind. Because I had sight for fourteen years, my dreams are visual. The people, places, and things in my dreams, the actions that take place, make visual impressions upon me, but I do not dream as one who can see. My dreams are much fuzzier and frequently mix discordant auditory and tactile impressions. They are not quite in tune with what I remember seeing before. In a dream I am a blind person in the world of the sighted—just as I am a blind person when I am awake.

I am sure my way of visualizing and dreaming cannot be experienced by the congenitally blind, those who have been blind all their lives. They do not have the memory of sight. My ways of observing, experiencing, and thinking are therefore based on an awareness of what objects look like, of differences in light and color. It is very important that my memory of sight enables me to grasp the abstract idea of a diagram or picture as an artificial representation of something else. As a result, my style of thinking and learning is closer to that of a seeing person than to that of someone who has never been able to see.

I do not deny that my blindness is often an inconvenience and a significant obstacle toward accomplishment of a goal, but prejudice causes me more frustration and anguish than blindness itself.

The importance of experiences missed by a blind person is often overestimated by the sighted. When I had partial vision, I saw the face of my wife, Kyoung, but I have never seen the faces of our children, Paul and Christopher. Some people say that I am thereby seriously deprived and express their pity in highly sentimental terms. I am told that Kyoung's face is very pretty and that both Paul and Chris are quite handsome, but I do not feel I am deprived as a husband and father just because I cannot see their faces.

I feel love in Kyoung's cheerful voice, her soft hands, her giving body, her caring personality. I especially like her voice—full of optimism, humor, caring, zest, and joy. I confess that it is important to me that she has a pretty face, because I enjoy the thought that she is attractive in the terms of people who can see. Beauty is not just visual. You can hear beauty. You can smell it. Beauty often transcends sensory experience. There is beauty in loving and feeling loved. Despite my blindness, I have many ways of "seeing" beauty.

I sense the children's love in the sound of their happy laughter, in watching them grow and develop intellectually and psychosocially, and in observing their personality differences.

Paul, now fourteen years old and heading into the ninth grade, has been given many talents by God. He is intellectually gifted; he participated in the Northwestern University Midwest Talent Search, taking the Scholastic Aptitude Test. As a result, he was chosen to take courses in Physics and Math Problem Solving with Computers in Purdue University's Star Program; Computer Science, Introduction to Pascal at Northwestern. Those are special summer residential programs for selected, gifted junior high school students. He plays a violin in his school orchestra, is in the schools' Future Problem Solving program, and is crazy about baseball in spring and summer, basketball in winter. He is popular with his peers and was elected a student council representative. He wants to go to Harvard University Medical or Law School.

Paul's personality is most like his mother's. He is compassionate, optimistic, humorous, cheerful, and outgoing. When he was in grade school, he used to give up one of his recesses to assist a special education teacher as a volunteer. His attitude toward my blindness is excellent. He does not mind having a father who is blind; in fact, he wishes to invent a car that blind people could drive. He knows much more than I about the Apple IIe computer which we have at home, so he is my computer teacher. With Braille and speech output devices, I have equal access to it.

Chris, who is eleven and going into sixth grade, has already been identified as gifted and talented. He sings in our church choir and plays the piano; he also plays saxophone in his school band. He has been enrolled in the program for gifted and talented students at Purdue University/Calumet as well as at his own school. His academic skills are most impressive—he scored in the ninety-ninth percentile on the Iowa Test of Basic Skills for three consecutive years. He is confident that he will go to Stanford or Princeton University and become a scientist. He tells us not to worry about his university expenses because he is sure he will win a full scholarship. I admire his confidence and ambition, but I try to teach him that how he lives his given life is more important than what he will be. His thinking is reflected in an essay he wrote for his school newsletter, "If I were the president of the U.S.A., I would ban all the guns and other weapons except for police, prevent any nuclear war by making a friendship treaty with the U.S.S.R., and keep world peace with cooperation of leaders of the other countries."

Chris's personality traits are more like mine. He strongly believes what is said in Deuteronomy 28:13, "And the LORD will make you the head, and not the tail; and you shall tend upward only, and not downward; if you obey the commandments of the LORD your God, which I command you this day, being careful to do them."

Both Paul and Chris do not hesitate to name their father as the person they most respect. We have excellent father-son relationships. In Paul's words, "Even though my father is blind, he does almost everything for us. He goes swimming and skating with us. He helps us to do our homework and teaches us not to give up before we try. He does not ski now; however, he has learned how to ski. The pictures of him skiing are fascinating. He is special to us."

I cannot hide my blindness, and I must live in a world run by those who are not blind. That means I must cope with the prejudice of people who do not like to be reminded that my fate could befall them. Sometimes such people react negatively when confronted by someone who cannot see. The negative reactions I have most often encountered are:

—Your blindness is a punishment for sin.
—In the face of your blindness, I feel helpless, uncomfortable, ill-at-ease.
—I reject you and your blindness; I avoid you.
—I am ashamed and in despair because I cannot cope with your being different.

Interestingly enough, some of those negative reactions are based on Scripture. Some biblical wrongdoers, for instance, were struck blind. In the Old Testament (Gen. 19:9–11) the Sodomites who came to assault Lot were blinded by two angels, and Lot escaped. In Leviticus 26:14–16, when Moses was given the injunction to obey the commandments, he was warned that dimming sight was one of the prices of transgression. Moses passed the warning on in his concluding charge to his people (Deut. 28:65). Samson was blinded by the Philistines (Judges 16:21) because he was a criminal in their eyes. Blindness as a punishment is mentioned twice in the book of Job (9:24; 29:15). Other moral injunctions backed by a threat of blindness are found in Psalm 69:23 and Proverbs 30:17.

Jesus of Nazareth saw blindness differently. As he passed by (John 9:1–3), Jesus saw a man blind from his birth. And his disciples asked him, "Rabbi, who sinned, this man or his parents, that he was born blind?" Jesus answered, "It was not that this man sinned, or his parents, but that the works of God might be made manifest in him."

In the Bible blind people are often characterized as groping, stumbling, or unable to find their way. The blind are among those disqualified from the priesthood (Lev. 21:16–23). Deuteronomy 28:28–29 thunders, "The LORD will smite you with madness and blindness and confusion of mind; and you shall grope at noonday, as the blind grope in darkness, and you shall not prosper in your ways."

In the Old Testament the blind are rejected. For example, in 2 Samuel 5:8 it is written, "The blind and the lame shall not come into the house," but in the New Testament, Jesus said, "But when you give a feast, invite the poor, the maimed, the lame, the blind, and you will be blessed, because they cannot repay you. You will be repaid at the resurrection of the just" (Luke 14:13–14).

In short, attitudes about the blind are diametrically opposed in the Old Testament and the New. Jesus denied the idea that blindness is a punishment for sin and instead emphasized mercy and compassion. It is due to his insight that the church has played an important role in the development of special education and rehabilitation for the blind and others.

The physical reality of my blindness frustrates me at times, to be sure, but the frequency and intensity of that frustration is less than that caused by prejudice and negative reaction. Let me share some particularly disturbing experiences.

If there were any single reason I wish I could see, it would be so that I could drive a car. I would like to go home from work without having to rely on Kyoung. She, too, has a demanding career teaching visually handicapped students. I would like to get back and forth by taking the bus, but there is no public bus in our town. We settled here because this town has a very good public school system and is located fairly close to Chicago, home of Northeastern Illinois University where I teach. When we resided in Pittsburgh during my graduate study, the bus was our only means of transport—except for an occasional ride with friends. I got back and forth from the university without Kyoung's help. I even ran her errands when she was ill or the children monopolized her time. Usually I enjoyed being independent and taking the bus, but from time to time the trip could get tense, even humiliating.

Between our apartment and the bus there were some scary streets to cross. Then there was the problem of identifying the bus. Several different bus routes shared my bus stop. In Seoul, public buses run very close together, but in Pittsburgh, if I missed a bus I had to wait half an hour. I stayed close to the buildings, carefully avoiding the curb and the loud, angry, rushing traffic. When I heard a bus, I would seek a Good Samaritan to identify it for me. Half the time I lost my Good Samaritan—his or her bus came first. I would then look for another.

Waiting on good days was a pleasure, but cold winter days were difficult. One very cold day I finally boarded the bus, coins in hand. I missed the coin box, my money dropped to the floor. My hands were so cold they were numb. I felt like an idiot. I imagined everyone laughing at me.

Driving a car is not the only thing I miss. I wish many things. I wish I could play baseball with Paul and Christopher, play tennis with Kyoung. She has relatively good psychomotor skills. She plays tennis—but not well. Playing with her would be much fun. Paul and Chris enjoy baseball, and they ask me to watch them play during the season. I usually find a good excuse but occasionally am talked into going to a game. I find it totally boring and frustrating. It makes me feel blind—or like the popular image of the blind.

One day shortly after a school term began, Paul jokingly asked me, "Will you coach our team?"

"No!" I replied.

"I mean our Future Problem Solving team," Paul said.

Feeling guilty because I cannot coach baseball, I am trying to make up by being a great Future Problem Solving coach. Last spring our team was invited to the state competition by placing third among almost five hundred teams dealing with the problem of artificial intelligence.

I wish I could pick up a book and read it when I want to or need to. I appreciate Braille, taped and talking books, and the live readers who are truly blessings, but I am frustrated by my inability to read when I want to. How wonderful it is to have three members of my family near when I need their vision.

In Korea there is legal discrimination. For example, the disabled cannot take examinations to become civil servants or to practice certain professions. No legal inequities or discrimination exists in the United States, to my knowledge, but a lot of negative reaction makes blindness much more frustrating.

In August of 1973, when I completed my master's degree work and was accepted to the Ph.D. program, we decided to find a larger apartment. We needed more room for our baby, Paul. Kyoung spent several days looking. Finally, she located an apartment that was just fine; she signed a lease and put down a hundred dollar deposit. She did not tell the landlord I was blind, never imagining it would matter.

The apartment was close enough to campus that I could walk every day. I was very pleased. Kyoung was eager to show it to me, so as soon as we had finished packing we bundled up Paul and went to the new address. When the landlord saw the three of us coming, he came out and, of course, discovered I was blind. Without saying anything, he rushed into the house and came out with Kyoung's one hundred dollars in hand. He was convinced—and he tried to convince me—that I would not be able to walk up and down the stairs. I was so angry I yelled at him, but I could not change his mind. Deep inside, he was convinced blindness was synonymous with helplessness. I know I would have won the case if I had taken it to court, but we bowed out, knowing that it could no longer be a happy place to live.

Blindness can be humiliating. One spring day in 1973, a few

weeks before Paul was born, Kyoung asked me to accompany her to the grocery. I was busy preparing for a final exam, but I went to help carry the groceries. While she shopped, I waited outside, reviewing in quiet concentration the subject matter of the coming examination. Suddenly I felt something drop into my pocket. Curious, I reached inside. As soon as my right hand entered my pocket, I identified a dime and a nickel. I assumed someone had taken me for a blind beggar.

I was outraged. I was no beggar. I considered myself quite elite, and I had many friends who concurred. I fumed. When Kyoung came out of the store, I said, "Honey, beggars in the United States must be very well dressed." My remark totally confused her.

"Well," I said, "I'm wearing a suit and a tie. I never, in the years when I still had my sight, saw a well-dressed beggar in Korea, but someone just made me a blind beggar by dropping fifteen cents into my pocket!"

Kyoung burst into laughter. "You have earned fifteen cents," she said. "That is the exact amount necessary to make a copy of the three-page article you need."

I was cheered by her optimism, by the eternal uplift of her personality, and we laughed our way home.

Blindness can be embarrassing. On one rainy day I was on my way home from a class required in my doctoral program. My ears were not as sensitive as usual because it was raining very hard. There were big puddles here and there. I was walking briskly, alternating my cane from left to right, less cautious than usual because, surely, no one would be standing still in such a downpour. Suddenly, inadvertently, unknowingly, I plunged the cane to the pavement between a lady's legs. "Are you blind?" she roared.

I apologized profusely and assured her I really was blind.

"Oh, you poor dear thing," she said sincerely—and sentimentally. But my pride was hurt, so I replied, "You need not be sorry for me. I am working on a doctoral degree, and my accomplishments have been inspirational to sighted people!"

Positive psychological experiences in blindness exist as well. Sometimes I am admired, and I confess I enjoy that.

I have observed there are cultural differences in positive attitudes toward blindness. First, it is more pronounced in equalitarian than in authoritarian cultures. Favorable attitudes toward many more things seem to exist where society is characterized by cooperation and democracy rather than dispassionate competition and absolute authority.

In Korea widespread belief maintains that blind people are especially suited to be soothsayers and seers because blindness is associated with mystery and magic. The blind are believed to have magical power among some groups of people—Vietnam, the northern tribes of Africa, and the North American Indians. The correlation of magic with blindness seems to be related to the belief that loss of vision is compensated by other gifts, by the increased power of other senses. Unfortunately, one's other senses do not automatically become sharp due to loss of vision; rather, blind people learn to better utilize their remaining senses through formal and informal training. The belief that the blind are particularly suited to be soothsayers and seers has directly and indirectly influenced the lives of the Korean blind. It is a detrimental belief for two reasons: (1) blind people themselves think they are useless for other occupations, so they do not challenge these beliefs to achieve a better life; (2) intelligent people, including government officials, know that fortune-telling is a superstition. They relegate the blind to a noncompetitive field by perpetuating the myth.

Korea was ruled by Japan for thirty-six years, from 1910 to 1945. During that period, Japan introduced massage into the vocational education curriculum at the Seoul School for the Blind, creating another image for Korean blind persons—the traditional blind masseur.

I entered the school for the blind after my accident, but I

rejected the roles of blind soothsayer and masseur. My hatred of those images motivated me to look for ways to go to college. One day in a massage class I whispered to my massage partner, "I will never become a masseur!" The teacher overheard. Upset, he scolded me by quoting an old Korean saying: he who spits at the well will be the first to drink water from it. I have been trying to disprove that saying ever since.

To the best of my knowledge, no accredited schools train blind persons to become soothsayers. They are trained individually through private tutoring or in small group lessons.

Other cultural differences exist in the way blind people are treated in Korea and in the United States, but Korea has more instances of rejection, and the degree of rejection is much more severe. When I was a high school student, I was occasionally pushed out of a public bus because of the superstition that seeing a blind person in the morning brings bad luck for the rest of the day. I am very proud of being an alumnus of Yonsei University, but I will never forget that my first application to the university was rejected solely because I was blind. Nor can I forget that at Yonsei, a Christian school promoting freedom and truth, when I wanted to join a student club, none of them accepted me.

Yes, there were some bad times. On some occasions, however, my blindness led to unexpected benefits.

My blindness is a handicap only when I let it be a handicap. It elicits favorable and unfavorable reactions from people who can see. When those reactions are negative, I feel handicapped; when they are positive, I feel exalted.

The personalities and abilities of people who can see are varied and unique. So are those of the blind. It is wrong to label any individual, to make anyone a stereotype. Blind persons have little in common except that they happen to be blind. Individuals, their talents, interests, appearance, circumstances, and philosophies are different. They are human beings before they are blind. Treatment of the blind should be based on human dignity and equal rights.

I do not live in a world of darkness, although I am totally blind. I forget, most of the time, that I am blind, and I am not even aware of being different. Perhaps more accurately, I do not mind being different.

I feel most grateful to God for a life that enables me to enjoy so many things. I strongly believe the day will come when my blindness will be a symbol of light to many people. I expect that miracle and strive toward its accomplishment. My efforts will never cease. When I stumble, I will keep my inner eye on the talents given to me, especially the talent to love and to be loved. On this planet, there is none so rich, so healthy, so powerful, or so strong that he or she does not need love. It is love that makes our world—seen or unseen—bright.

Sometimes, somebody will say to me, "You must be brilliant." I am not brilliant. What it took to get me through college, through a master's program, and on to my doctorate was not genius but the help and support, prayers and money of many people who invested in me and my family. On my part, it took eight or ten grinding hours a day, reviewing tapes, tracing Braille, listening to readers. I am not different from sighted people except that I cannot see, but I do seem to have received a talent from God to inspire others. I can do much more with this ability than with any intellectual ability I may have. I am not rich or powerful, but I can inspire the disabled to seek rehabilitation and the nondisabled to seek justice and equal rights for the handicapped. From personal experience, I have learned that rehabilitation comes through inspiration, from hope. What I want to do the rest of my life is to continue to build bridges of hope between the disabled and nondisabled—with God's help.

Postscript
A Special Word

I COULD NOT END my story without a special word of thanks to and recognition of an organization that brings hope to so many people all over the world and is an integral part of anything I have achieved—the Rotary International and its Foundation.

My Rotary connection goes back to when I first came to the United States in 1972 to work on my master's degree. William T. Powell was then governor of Rotary District 728 in northwestern Pennsylvania. His district, as its international service project, paid for my travel and living expenses for one year. In addition, Mr. Powell obtained a full tuition scholarship for me from the University of Pittsburgh through my academic adviser, Dr. Ralph Peabody. When I was accepted to the Ph.D. program in 1973, I was awarded a Rotary Foundation scholarship that covered our living expenses for another year.

In January of 1981, Mr. Powell wrote suggesting I would make a good Rotarian. I saw it as an opportunity to increase international understanding and to promote equal rights and full participation for disabled persons in and through Rotary. When the Rotary Club of Munster, IN, invited me to join, I was quick to accept, and I have been an active Rotarian ever since, chairing the club's international service and community service committees.

Our international committee in 1984 successfully completed a Rotary Foundation special grant project, sending cassette book machines and talking calculators to thirteen schools for the blind in Korea. The book machines will accept specially taped books from the Library of Congress and other sources. Talking calculators help teach math concepts to blind persons. The project helped build a bridge between handicapped and nonhandicapped, enhanced international understanding of rehabilitation, sensitized the public to the needs and potential of the disabled, and improved the quality of education of the blind in Korea.

As another international service project, the Munster Rotary Club had five thousand copies of A Light in My Heart printed in Korean. It was distributed to ophthalmologists and their recently blinded patients and to selected civic and government leaders. Contributions to the project came also from the Rotary Foundation of Rotary International and other clubs. After reading the book, Dr. Byung Woo Kong, the first Korean ophthalmologist and the inventor of the Korean typewriter, donated eighty typewriters toward rehabilitation of the blind. A second edition of the book was printed by the Christian Broadcasting System in Seoul and sold in Christian bookstores throughout Korea. Taegu University Braille Library has published an edition for the blind.

The seventy-fourth Rotary International Convention was held in Toronto June 5–9, 1983. A special guest among seventeen thousand convention participants, I was asked to speak at the Paul Harris Luncheon on "International Understanding Through Rehabilitation."

Guests were quiet as I told them, "As a recipient of the Rotary Foundation Scholarship, I am greatly indebted to the Rotary for my own rehabilitation, and as a Rotarian I am promoting the welfare and mainstreaming of the disabled.

"The primary goal of rehabilitation is to prevent disability from becoming a handicap. Disability may be an advantage or a handicap, depending on the situation. Disability becomes a handicap when it is a significant obstacle to the accomplishment of a goal, when it serves as a negative stimulus to others, or when it negates the effectiveness of the body as a tool for action.

"My blindness was a negative stimulus to others in Korea. Even in the United States, blindness sometimes generates negative attitudes, but in Asia, prejudice, discrimination, and negativism are much worse. There is even a superstition that merely seeing a blind person in the morning will bring bad luck all day. Because of these prejudices, my blindness was a handicap, but it is no longer.

"With the help of many people and especially Rotary, I was able to prevail over ancient prejudices, official roadblocks, and the absence of easy help. The Rotary Club has played an enormous part in my rehabilitation and in my life.

"During graduate study at the University of Pittsburgh under Rotary auspices, I was frequently invited to speak to various Rotary clubs and at the district conference, and I learned firsthand of the compassion of Rotarians, the kind of compassion that is essential to rehabilitation."

Then I told the assembled guests of the Rotary Foundation special grant project to aid each of the thirteen Korean schools for the blind, and of the Young Woo Kang Scholarship Foundation at Taegu University to promote the welfare and higher education of blind students in Korea. I told them how in my teaching and speaking I was able to help both the blind and sighted to have insight into the capacities and possibilities of the blind as well as into their special problems.

I closed the speech with the prayer of an unknown Confederate soldier, a prayer that has become my own:

> I asked God for strength that I might achieve. I was made weak that I might learn humbly to obey.
>
> I asked for health that I might do greater things. I was given infirmity that I might do better things.
>
> I asked for riches that I might be happy. I was given poverty that I might be wise.

I asked for power that I might get the praise of men. I was given weakness that I might feel the need of God.

I asked for all things that I might enjoy life. I was given life that I might enjoy all things.

I got nothing that I had asked for, but everything that I had hoped for.

The sixteen hundred Paul Harris Fellows in attendance gave Kyoung and me a standing ovation. The chairman of the Rotary Foundation trustees, James Bomar, Jr., presented me with the Rotary Foundation Citation for Meritorious Service, recognizing my efforts for the furthering of better understanding and friendly relations among peoples of the world.

I was invited to speak before thirty-four Rotary clubs and districts in four nations. In the year after the Harris Fellow speech, I spoke to approximately sixty thousand people at seventy-four occasions—Rotary groups, churches of many denominations, high schools, universities, special education teachers, rehabilitation workers, prisoners.

Then in 1983 I had the wonderful opportunity to invite William Powell to speak at Taegu University and to be his interpreter. Dr. Tae Young Rhee, president of Taegu University, arranged for us to meet with the Korean ministers of Education and Social Affairs. As Pennsylvania State Welfare Administrator, Mr. Powell had much expertise to share with them, and these meetings, the highlight of our trip, made an impact on Korean policy-making toward the disabled. Mr. Powell's lectures also made a deep impression on the students and faculty of Taegu University. His theme is one of the themes of my life as well as of the Rotary Club: "rehabilitation is a good investment."